CONTENTS

INTRODUCTION

Note: County/Area

Although in some parts of the British Isles, Scout Counties are known as Areas or Islands, in one case Bailiwick, and from 1 April 2008 in Scotland, a Region, for ease of reading this resource we simply refer to County or Counties.

INTRODUCTION

Planning a programme that is interesting and enjoyable for the young people in your Troop can be difficult. The pressures of time and work can make it harder still to come up with good ideas. *The Troop Programme Plus* is made up of a selection of practical programme ideas, games and skill instructions to help you plan your programme. Whether you are a new Leader or someone who has been involved for many years, this resource will provide you with new ideas for those evenings when you are short of inspiration.

The Troop Programme Plus provides about a year's worth of meetings, divided into three terms of ten weeks. You may of course meet more or less than this, but the idea is that the programmes here can be adapted to suit your circumstances. All the types of programme covered in *The Troop Programme* have been incorporated in the ideas that follow, to help you use a wide range in your meetings. Before the detailed programmes for each term, a summary is there to give you an overview of zones visited, Methods used, and badges linked to. There is also a checklist of things the Section Leader needs to do, and a list of other people you may need to contact to prepare for the term ahead.

This resource has been written to complement two others: *Troop Essentials* is a manual to help you with your role as Section Leader, Assistant or Helper. It is the indispensable guide to running a Scout Troop and will tell you all you need to know about your Section and your role within it. The Troop Programme explains the broader Balanced Programme and helps you plan and deliver programmes for your Section. It will provide you with many of the tools, ideas and techniques needed to run an exciting Balanced Programme for your Troop.

The Troop Programme Plus is essentially the paper counterpart to Programmes Online (POL), the popular online resource for programme material. Programmes Online can be found at www.scouts.org.uk/pol – Members of The Scout Association can sign up to access a database of programme ideas, many of which have been suggested by Leaders around the country. We hope you will use this book to help plan your programme, and get inspiration from programme ideas that definitely work. To keep your programme fresh, Programmes Online is the ideal companion, with ideas being regularly contributed by Leaders just like you! **www.scouts.org.uk/pol**

POL

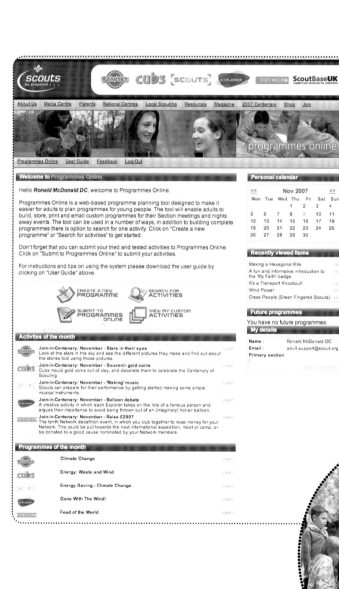

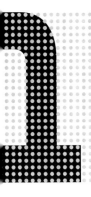

PROGRAMME PLAN TERM 1

WELCOME TO *THE TROOP PROGRAMME PLUS*. IT IS A RESOURCE THAT HELPS YOU PLAN YOUR PROGRAMMES. THE FIRST TERM COVERS ALL OF THE PROGRAMME ZONES AND WORKS TOWARDS FOUR OF THE CHALLENGES, COMPLETING THE ADVENTURE CHALLENGE AND THE CREATIVE CHALLENGE.

Scouting Skills covered include route planning, compass skills, pioneering and camp cooking.

You will spend at least one Night Away and complete one Hike Away. Six of the programmes involve visits or visitors and you will need to arrange extra adult help on five occasions.

This term you will link with the Cub Section and invite parents to the final meeting of term. During weeks 3-5 you will meet at different locations (not the Meeting Place). Unusual items you may need to purchase in advance are half-cut drainpipes, planks of wood, and old greetings cards.

Week	Programme	Zone	Method
1	Time traveller	F / OA / BA	G / TBA / AO
2	Cricket with Cubs	F	G / TBA / PWR
3	Patrol Activities - Adventure Challenge	OA / F / BA	AwO / TNS / PWR
4	Patrol Activities - Adventure Challenge	OA / F / BA	AwO / TNS / PWR
5	Patrol Activities - Adventure Challenge	OA / F / BA	AwO / TNS / PWR
6	A song and a dance 1	CE / C	VV / DC
7	A song and a dance 2	CE / OA	DC / TNS / PWR
7b	Concert at an old people's home	C / CE / BA	S / DC
8	Incident hike	OA / CE / F	AO / TBA
9	Global programme – free healthcare	G / BA	T / G / AwO
10	Camp Cooking Challenge	OA / CE	TBA / VV

Key – Zones			
OA	Outdoor and Adventure	CE	Creative Expression
F	Fit for Life	G	Global
C	Community	BA	Beliefs and Attitudes
Key – Methods			
G	Games	AO	Activities outdoors
T	Themes	AwO	Activities with others
TBA	Team building activities	PWR	Prayer, worship and reflection
S	Service	VV	Visits and visitors
DC	Design and creativity	TNS	Technology and new skills

PROGRAMME METHODS

PROGRAMME ZONES	Activities Outdoors	Games	Design & creativity	Visits & visitors	Service	Technology & new skills	Team building activities	Activities with others	Themes	Prayer worship & reflection
Outdoor & Adventure	✓	✓		✓		✓	✓	✓		
Global		✓						✓	✓	
Community			✓	✓	✓					
Fit for Life	✓	✓	✓	✓			✓	✓		
Creative Expression			✓	✓						
Beliefs & Attitudes									✓	✓

The Bottom Line

Activity ○○○ Fun ○○○ Teamwork ○○○ Leadership ○○○ Relationships ○○○ Commitment ○○○ Personal development ○○○

1 tick = Poor
2 ticks = Good
3 ticks = Excellent

BADGES WORKED TOWARDS THIS TERM

CONTACTS FOR THIS TERM'S PROGRAMME:

Cub Scout Leader
Cricket with Cubs

District Commissioner
Activity approval

Activity providers
(e.g. diving instructor, campsite office) – Book activities, arrange dates

Old people's home
Offer service element and arrange details of concert

Help the Aged worker
Invite for visit to talk to Scouts about their work

Dance/singing coach
To teach songs/dance

Scout campsite
Book pitch for the Camp Cooking Challenge

CHECKLIST FOR TERM 1 PROGRAMME

- Book campsite activities for term. ○
- Book external providers. ○
- Arrange date for old people's home concert. ○
- Organise dates for visitor to come (Help the Aged/creative tutors). ○
- Write letters for Adventure Challenge. ○
- Write parent letter for Camp Cooking Challenge. ○
- Check equipment stores and purchase any equipment needed. ○
- Re-stock First Aid kit. ○
- Arrange extra adult help for programmes 3, 4, 5, 7b and 8. ○
- Order badges from Badge Secretary. ○

WEEK 1 – TIME TRAVELLER

Throughout your time as a Section Leader, you will find there is much to be learned from other Leaders and programmes that have worked well in the past. This programme, run in a traditional style, takes ideas from *Scouting* magazines from the past 60 years.

Programme Zones:	Fit for life, Outdoor and Adventure, Beliefs and Attitudes
Methods:	Games, Team building activities, Activities outdoors
Preparation time:	20-30 minutes to set up obstacle course; 4 adults to run bases x 10 minutes each
Location	Indoor bases/Outdoor obstacle course

You will need

- Old Christmas cards (cut in halves)
- Scissors
- Hand drill
- Three hooks (attached to wall)
- Lightweight tent in bag
- Hand axe
- Labels
- Steel spring clips
- Toolbox
- Union Flag
- Staffs (one per Patrol)
- Full use of equipment stores to construct obstacle course (poles, lashing ropes, chairs, etc.)

Time	Activity				Additional Information	Run by
Before	Coming in game – Fizz Buzz					Young Leaders
19:00	Opening ceremony/flag break/inspection (record books)				Flag break done by duty Patrol	
19:15	Game – Christmas Card Match-up					
	Activities and Training - bases					
	Bulldogs	Woodpeckers	Eagles	Tigers		
19:30	Rope making	Blindfold tent-pitching	Know that axe	Flag folding		
19:45	Blindfold tent-pitching	Know that axe	Flag folding	Rope making		
20:00	Know that axe	Flag folding	Rope making	Blindfold tent-pitching		
20:15	Flag folding	Rope making	Blindfold tent-pitching	Know that axe		
20:30	Game – Doodle Bug				Tidy up bases while playing	
20:40	Patrol Competition – Horse and Rider				Leaders to supervise each obstacle as agreed in Risk Assessment.	All
20:58	Quick fall-in/notices/flag down					

ACTIVITY DETAILS

Fizz Buzz

- The Troop sits in a circle.

- The idea is to count clockwise around the circle, each player shouting a number in turn. However any number divisible by three must be replaced with the word 'fizz' and any number divisible by four must be replaced with the word 'buzz'.

- For a number divisible by both three and four the player must shout 'fizz-buzz'.

- Example: one, two, fizz, buzz, five, fizz, seven, buzz, fizz, ten, eleven, fizz-buzz and so on…

- For best enjoyment, play the game fast. Any players hesitating or making a wrong call go out (or accrue O.U.T. until they are out).

There are various alternative ways of playing the game, such as changing the factor number you call 'fizz' or 'buzz' on. You can also use four and six and cricketing gestures; using a rhythm and actions to make the game even more fun. Your Scouts will devise their own rules as they get more confident with the game.

Christmas Card Match-up

- You will need about three times as many old cards as Scouts.

- Cut each card into two pieces, making two sets of half-cards, so that one set has its counterpart in the other.

- Cut the cards in different ways, making some halves easy to identify and some more tricky.

- Distribute one set of half-cards all over the Meeting Place. Hide some, make some easy to find.

- Give each Scout one half-card from the other set, keeping a pool of spares in your hand.

- On the word 'Go' the Scouts set about finding the card that matches the one you gave them. On finding a pair, the Scout returns to you with it, and receives another card from you.

- Completed pairs are placed in the Patrol's corner. At the end of the game (an agreed time limit or when all the pairs have been found) the Patrol with the largest number of paired pieces wins.

Rope Making

Try making your own ropes from string. Start with three strings attached at one end to hooks. Put their other ends on a hook placed in a hand drill chuck. Turning the drill will wind the strings together. Seal each end with a whipping.

Blindfold Tent Pitching

- Using lightweight tents that your Scouts are used to camping in, Patrols work together under the guidance of the Patrol Leader to pitch these tents wearing blindfolds (use scarves for these, not plastic bags).

- Give them a time limit in which to finish, then let them assess how successful they were.

- Try this again later in the year after you have done some camping to see how much they improve.

Know that Axe

A good way of teaching the Troop the different parts of an axe is by displaying it in the Meeting Place, with tags labelling the haft, the toe and so on. If you use steel spring clips, the axe can be easily taken down to use. Remember to keep it masked when not in use.

To test your Scouts' knowledge, change the tags around so that they are wrong, and see how long it takes for an eagle-eyed Scout to notice. Spend the time on the base in this programme setting up a place to display the axe, and the rest of the time studying the parts in order to learn their names. Of course, learning how to use an axe is something that can only be taught in a practical way.

Flag Folding

- Set up a base near the flagpole, to show Scouts ways of folding the flag ready for flag break, as shown.

- While Scouts practice flag folding, explain the correct term for the flag (Union Flag not Union Jack); how to recognise when the flag is the right way up; how to break the flag correctly.

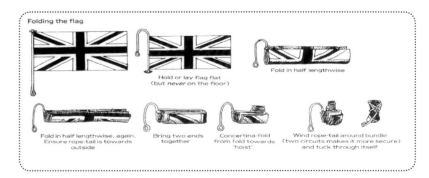

Folding the flag

Hold or lay flag flat (but *never* on the floor)

Fold in half lengthwise

Fold in half lengthwise, again. Ensure rope-tail is towards outside

Bring two ends together

Concertina-fold from fold towards 'hoist'

Wind rope-tail around bundle (two circuits makes it more secure) and tuck through itself

Doodle Bug

Patrols stand in file. A staff is placed opposite each Patrol at the far end of the room. The Patrol Leader runs to the staff, returns with it held horizontally at shoulder height. Meanwhile the rest of the Patrol duck down. The Patrol Leader runs alongside the Patrol holding the staff above their bowed heads. On reaching the back at the Patrol, the staff is brought down and held horizontally at knee height. The Patrol Leader runs alongside the Patrol once more, and the Scouts jump over the staff as it passes under them. The Patrol Leader returns the staff to its starting point, runs back, touches the next Scout and the race continues in the same manner.

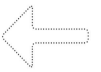
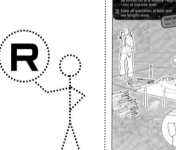

Horse and Rider

Build an obstacle course in the Meeting Place (or outside it) which is challenging but possible for a Scout to complete on another Scout's shoulders. Suggested obstacles are shown below.

Scouts split up in pairs within their Patrol groupings, and are told that they must attempt the course as horse and rider. The time they take to complete the course is noted and five seconds are added for each 'fault'. The faults are as follows

- Fences: knocking staves from chairs
- Stepping stones: touching the floor
- Slalom: touching the tubes
- Walk: touching the spars
- Water jump: falling off the plank
- Quoits: failing to lance the quoit at the first attempt
- Balloon: failing to burst the balloon after two attempts

The pair of Scouts with the fastest time at the end wins points for their Patrol.

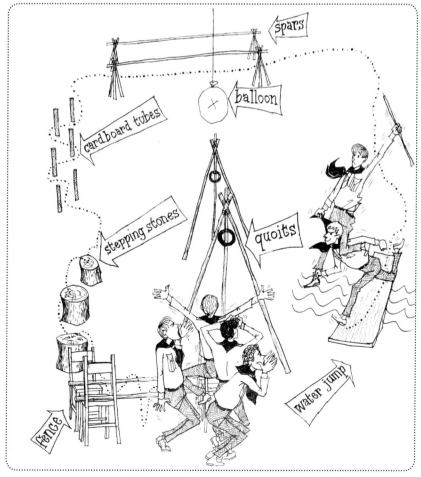

Horse and Rider

WEEK 2 - CRICKET WITH CUBS

Linking activities are a crucial part of Scouting. They encourage young people to understand their role as a member of the wider Movement and to continue when they come to the end of their time in one Section. They also provide Leaders of different Sections with an opportunity to get together and check that there is a flow and progression between the programmes, so that Members are being consistently challenged to take their achievements further when they move on.

This programme to run with Cubs is full of activity, teamwork and fun. You may have a different, favourite game that you would run as a linking event, but the principles here are what's really important.

Programme Zone:	Fit for Life
Methods:	Activities outdoors, Games, Team building activities
Links to badges:	None
Preparation time:	Setting up pitch - 5 minutes. Explaining rules and choosing teams - 10 minutes
Location:	Outdoors on playing field or park ground.

Time	Activity	Additional Information	Run by
19:00	Cubs and Scouts meet together at Meeting Place. Cubs opening ceremony followed by Scouts opening ceremony (break flag). Welcome Cubs to meeting. Leave for outdoor playing field.	Flag break done by duty Patrol	
19:30	Pick teams/Explain rules/Non-stop cricket	Teams should be mixed with Cubs/Scouts. Patrol Leader to be one captain, Sixer to be other captain.	
20:00	Switch batting/bowling team if not all out		
20:30	End of innings – announce winner!		
20:45	Return to Meeting Place/closing ceremony and short prayer		

ACTIVITY DETAILS

Non-stop Cricket

The rules are as follows:

- Scouts and Cubs are divided into equal teams by an appropriate method. One Cub Sixer is chosen to be captain of Team A and a Scout Patrol Leader is chosen to be captain of Team B. The captains toss a coin to decide who bats/fields.

- The pitch is set up as in the diagram opposite. The wicket is the facing side of a storage box/crate (one that makes a good sound when hit is best) and the batsman must run around a stump in line with the wicket and back to record one run. Running to the stump and hitting it with the bat does not count as a run.

- The batting team must sit quietly behind the wicket keeper and to one side for the duration of their inning. They must not interfere with the ball if it comes towards them, and runs can be deducted from their total for doing so.

- Only one run can be given when the ball is hit behind the batsman.

- You may choose not to run if you do not hit the ball.

- The bowler must bowl underarm, and hit the wicket without the ball bouncing. Overarm bowling is not allowed. Balls that bounce before hitting the stumps are not out. The bowler should bowl so that the ball passes the bat at a height that is judged to be above the knee but below the shoulder of the batsman. Balls outside this range are no-balls.

- Two no-balls bowled in succession result in a run to the batting team. If a bowler is repeatedly bowling no-balls, the umpire should use his/her discretion and consider replacing the bowler.

- Batting players can be bowled out and caught out. They can not be run out, as in conventional cricket.

- Bowlers must bowl from the bowling stump. Bowling from in front of it is considered a no-ball.

- A Leader will be assigned to each team to keep score. Scores should be kept secret, particularly in the second team's innings, when the young people will be anxious to know how close to the total they are. The announcement of the scores at the end of the match should be filled with suspense.

- Other rules may be introduced as favoured by your particular way of playing. These may include:

  - Compulsory 'get-out' rules for hitting the ball over walls, to the extremities of the playing field

  - Introducing boundaries (four or six) for exceeding the limits of the field of play

  - Catching rules to complicate the game, e.g. one bounce plus one-handed catch means out.

Notes

- The purpose of this programme is to promote links between the Sections and provide opportunities for Cubs and Scouts to work together. The Scouts of your Troop have a leading role to play in this, so encourage them to support the younger members of their team.

- Adults assigned to teams could bat for their teams, but should adapt their play accordingly so as not to injure youth members or play in too aggressive a manner. Adults should wait until all the young people in their team have batted.

- If you don't own suitable storage boxes as part of your Group equipment, you could adapt the game to involve bouncing a larger ball in between two stumps, use an upturned table with the wicket drawn out in chalk, or improvise!

A Cricketing Prayer

'Oh Lord if I must die today,
Please make it after close of play.
For this I know, if nothing more,
I will not go, without the score'

Sir John Major, Former Prime Minister

Thank you God for fun and games, which we can share together as Cubs and Scouts. Help us to enjoy the game of life, to get as many runs as we can, push the boundaries and know that everyone is an important member of the team.

Amen

Non-stop Cricket – Field of Play

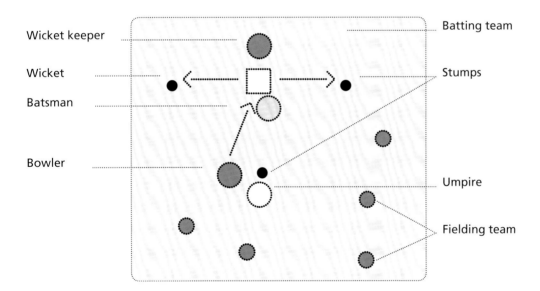

Wicket keeper

Wicket

Batsman

Bowler

Batting team

Stumps

Umpire

Fielding team

WEEKS 3-5 – ADVENTURE CHALLENGE

Adventure is what we provide for young people each week. A good programme needs good, adventurous activities to sustain the interest of today's young people - otherwise they leave. The Adventure Challenge can be used effectively to promote activities that require skill, determination and self-belief. This programme, run over three weeks, splits the Troop down into Patrols. If you run a smaller Troop, tackle the Challenge all together. You'll get just as much out of it…

You will need

- The activities A-Z, available at www.scouts.org.uk/activities
- Equipment required for activities chosen (if Scout led by members of your leadership team)
- Adventure Challenge badges to award at the end of the three weeks

Programme Zones:	Outdoor and Adventure; Fit for life; Beliefs and Attitudes
Methods:	Activities outdoors; Technology and new skills
Links to badges:	Adventure Challenge; Various Activity Badges (dependent on activities chosen)
Preparation time:	Depending on how you choose to run these activities, this can involve as little preparation time as a phone call to your local activity centre or campsite.
Location:	Activity Centre or Campsite, local swimming pool

Preparation

First you will need to decide which activities you wish to do towards the Adventure Challenge. The requirements list several, but the list is not exhaustive. A good starting place is the Activities A-Z available at www.scouts.org.uk/activities This outlines many activities and gives advice on organising them.

The next step is to hold a Troop or Patrol Forum so that the Scouts themselves decide what they would like to do. This will need to take place well in advance of the sessions themselves, so that you have plenty of time to book activities.

As you're splitting into Patrols to tackle these activities you will require more adult help than for a normal meeting. Patrol activities can be a fantastic opportunity to encourage parents to see just what their son or daughter gets up to at a Troop meeting. After seeing what fun they have, perhaps they'll be more likely to help more regularly. Be sure that all adults taking Scouts out have gone through the relevant record checks (See *Troop Essentials* page 22).

Timetable

This is a sample timetable of what the three weeks may look like:

ACTIVITY DETAILS

There is more than one way to run an adventurous activity, but you must adhere to the Adventurous Activity Permit Scheme. See *Troop Essentials* pages 35-36 for more details of what you need to do based on the activities you choose.

As each activity will need to be taken individually, you may find a checklist useful to make sure you have covered everything.

Also opposite is a template for a letter to send to parents in advance of the meetings, personalised by Patrol.

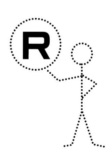

WEEK ONE		WEEK TWO		WEEK THREE	
District Campsite		**District Campsite**		**District Campsite**	
Bulldogs	High ropes	Kestrels	High ropes	Woodpeckers	High ropes
Woodpeckers	Climbing	Bulldogs	Climbing	Tigers	Climbing
Swimming Pool		**Swimming Pool**		**Swimming Pool**	
Kestrels	Sub aqua	Woodpeckers	Canoeing	Kestrels	Canoeing
Tigers	Canoeing	Tigers	Sub aqua	Bulldogs	Sub Aqua

Sample checklist for sub aqua, assuming this activity is commercially led (by local PADI club) and held at the local swimming pool (indoor):

1. Contact District Commissioner to gain approval. ○
2. Contact diving club to book session/instructor ○
   a. Check provider has relevant qualification ○
   b. Check provider has personal liability insurance ○
3. Ring pool to book sessions. ○
4. Make a record of start/finish times. ○
5. Arrange extra adult help. ○
6. Inform Scouts when they are doing which activity and times they start/finish. ○
7. Arrange transport to/from the activity (if local, this could involve informing parents of a different place to meet). ○

Sample checklist for climbing, assuming this activity is Scout led (by District Climbing Instructors) and held at District campsite.

1. Contact District Commissioner to get approval. ○
2. Contact Campsite office to book sessions and climbing instructors. ○
3. Complete Risk Assessment. ○
4. Arrange extra adult help. ○
5. Inform Scouts where/when they are doing which activity and times they start/finish. ○
6. Arrange transport to/from the activity (if local, this could involve informing parents of a different place to meet). ○

This is how a slip informing the Scouts/parents of the arrangements for Patrol Activities may look, which would be given one to two weeks prior to the activities taking place.

Example letter

Dear

From 25 March, the Troop will be working towards the Adventure Challenge, and taking part in some exciting activities. We will be splitting into Patrols for three weeks, with each Patrol doing a different activity each week. Because of this, we will not be meeting at the usual Meeting Place. Please read the table below to see where your son/daughter needs to be on which date.

Drew is in **Woodpeckers Patrol**

Date	Activity	Location	Start/finish
25 March	Climbing	Anytown Campsite, AB12 3CD	6:30/8:15
1 April	Canoeing	Anytown Swimming Pool, Station Road	7:00/9:00
8 April	High Ropes	Anytown Campsite, AB12 3CD	6:30/8:15

Please make arrangements to drop your daughter to the correct location on time. You may be able to arrange with other parents to share the driving so that you only have to drive one evening.

If you have any questions, I can always be contacted on my mobile – 07123 456789

Best wishes,

Hugh

Scout Leader, 1st Anytown Scouts

Badge link

Any Scouts attending all three weeks of the Patrol Activities will qualify for the Adventure Challenge.

Note

As well as providing challenge, fun and adventure, this programme provides opportunities for your Scouts to conquer fears, test their limits and build confidence. Completing a high ropes course brings with it a huge sense of achievement, and this is why the programme falls into the Beliefs and Attitudes Zone. You should try and build some element of reflection into the activity, so that Scouts are able to express their feelings about what they have done. This could be in the form of a display, presentation or ceremony. Awarding the badges is a good way to acknowledge how the Scouts developed by completing the activities.

WEEK 6 – A SONG AND A DANCE 1

Creative activities can be daunting for some members of the Troop (and some Leaders!) However overcoming doubts and stage fright can be as rewarding an experience as conquering vertigo or spending a week away from home.

Linking a concert performance to the Community Challenge and putting on a show at an old people's home is a great way to get everyone involved. The closeness of the activity to the Scout Promise makes it a lot more meaningful for the less theatrical Scouts and there is a role for everyone whether singing solo or working behind the scenes.

You will need

- A CD player
- Tables set up for Help the Aged presentation/game
- Keyboard
- Equipment from games list
- TV/Video or DVD (if required)

Programme Zones:	Community, Creative Expression
Methods:	Visits and visitors, Design and creativity.
Links to badges:	Community Challenge, Creative Challenge, Entertainer Activity Badge
Preparation time:	Prior arrangement with dance coach/singing teacher and Help the Aged visitor
Location:	Indoor

Time	Activity				Additional Information	Run by
19:00	Opening Ceremony				Change into activity clothes after flag break	
19:15	Drama game – What are you doing?				see page 86	
	Tigers	Eagles	Bulldogs	Woodpeckers		
19:25	Learn dance steps for the concert at old people's home – led by Yvonne from local dance school		Learn songs to sing at concert for old people's home – led by Akela from Cub Pack.		Reuben's dad is coming to play the songs on his keyboard. Can use upstairs room for this base. Yvonne will need big space and CD player.	
20:10	Game – active and rowdy					
20:25	Visit from care worker, to talk about care for the elderly		Needs TV and video for her presentation.			Gill from Help the Aged
20:55	Closing ceremony and flag down					

ACTIVITY DETAILS

This programme is highly suitable for working through a variety of awards and will present the Troop with a genuine challenge, and rewarding outcome. You should find it relatively simple to contact your nearest old people's home. They are normally very keen to have people (especially young people) coming in to perform to the residents.

- Unless one of your leadership team is skilled in dance or choreography, you would be best placed asking a tutor from a nearby dance school to come and teach the Troop some basic steps. Bear in mind who the audience is – they probably won't appreciate a heavy metal routine! Make a note of the steps so that you can rehearse again next week (unless the dance coach is returning!)

- Split the Troop in half, with one group learning the dance and the other contributing the songs. You could leave this up to choice, but it's better to keep Scouts in their Patrols as they will remain in these groupings for the Incident Hike in week eight. This doesn't mean there can't be a few swaps, but you'll need to keep a record so that they stay in their groups next week.

- Choose songs that the residents will be familiar with, but that the Scouts will enjoy singing too. It's better to choose upbeat ones, so that the audience is picked up by the performance on the day. Good examples are 'Come Fly with Me' and 'Rock around the Clock' – your Scouts may have some good suggestions too. Print out the lyrics to the songs before the meeting so that the singers have them to take home and practice. The tune should stick in their minds more easily.

Visit from care worker

The aim of this half hour is for the Scouts to learn something about care for the elderly, and the centre they will be visiting to perform the concert later in the term.

- You will have arranged for the care worker to come with activities planned; hopefully these will involve some sort of game or visual exercise, video or DVD.

- At the end of the session, encourage the Scouts to ask questions and find out more about where they will be going so that they know what to expect.

- Though this activity will be run by the visitor, be on hand to keep the Troop listening and provide support where it is asked for.

Organisations working with the elderly

- AGE Concern

- Help the Aged - We will

- Sue Ryder Care

Badge links

Community Challenge, Creative Challenge

Your performance may not be as spectacular as this, but you get the idea!

WEEK 7 – A SONG AND A DANCE 2

This programme allows the Troop to practice their concert for the residents of an old people's home. It will also help them learn some Scouting skills for the following week's incident hike. This programme uses a half-matrix structure and assumes that two Patrols are involved in singing and two Patrols in dancing at the concert. Scouts will need to be in the same Patrols for the incident hike.

You will need
- Compasses
- Maps
- Route cards (see appendix)
- Musical accompaniment (for song and dance)
- CD player
- Pencils/paper

Programme Zones:	Creative Expression, Outdoor and Adventure
Methods:	Design and creativity, Technology and new skills, Activities with others
Links to badges:	Creative Challenge, Entertainer Activity Badge
Preparation time:	Recap dance steps and song lyrics before meeting, Scouting Skills bases will need setting up (10 minutes each); this programme requires at least three base leaders.
Location:	Troop Meeting Place (Compass skills base ideally run outside Meeting Place)

Time	Activity				Additional Information	Run by
19:00	Opening Ceremony					
	Woodpeckers	Bulldogs	Tigers	Eagles		
19:25	Rehearsal of songs for the old people's home concert		Route planner for Incident Hike	Compass skills	Need keyboard (Reuben's dad)	
19:35			Compass skills	Route planner for Incident Hike		
20:00	Route planner for Incident Hike	Compass Skills	Rehearsal of dance for the old people's home concert		Need CD player with music for dance	
20:20	Compass Skills	Route planner for Incident Hike				
20:45	Closing ceremony/notices/flag down				Give out details of next week's incident hike	

ACTIVITY DETAILS

Song and dance rehearsals

The main aim of these longer sessions is to ensure that the Troop is prepared for their concert at the old people's home (which you have already arranged for the forthcoming weekend).

- You will need to go over the songs and dance moves that have been taught the previous week.

- Note that some Scouts will be less coordinated and have not been able to remember the words/ steps. Try and give extra support to those that need it, while allowing the more able Scouts to perfect their parts and perhaps coach others.

- Partnering more able Scouts with ones that are struggling is a good idea, as they can encourage each other so that everyone is confident.

- Because this is a longer session, you can adopt a more flexible approach. Roughly 45 minutes is plenty of time to refresh everyone's memory and have a few run-throughs.

- Build confidence by being positive at the conclusion of the rehearsal and excited about the concert.

Badge links

This activity goes towards the Creative Challenge (performing) requirement and the Entertainer Activity Badge, which can both be completed once the performance is given.

COMPASS SKILLS

In preparation for the Incident Hike, a 20 minute base on compass skills will test the Scouts' navigation. It will also give them an extra skill to be put to practical use next week. If you meet less than five minutes from a natural high point or open space, this base is best run outside. All you will then need is a table and a selection of local maps and a compass per Scout.

Instructions

- For beginners, explain the basic parts and functions of the compass: that it is used to navigate between two fixed points by giving you a bearing to walk on; that it uses the compass points (N, E, S, W) and relates each to a three-figure bearing from 000°-360°.

- Give the Patrol the task of orientating the map (so that north on their compass equates to north on the map) – once they think they have done this, look at it and give tuition if needed.

- Instruct Scouts how to find a bearing between two points on the map (even better if you can see them, e.g. Meeting Place and church with tower) – give them two more points to find bearings for them using map and compass.

Note: You may not have time to cover all these activities depending on the ability/knowledge of the Scouts.

Resources: The Scout Skills factsheet *Compass* (FS 315074) provides useful information on using a compass. You could also incorporate the Scouts' Skills Card in this activity, as it comes with grid references to use and features to find bearings of.

ROUTE PLANNER FOR INCIDENT HIKE

By the end of this base, the Patrol should have worked out their route for the following week's incident hike. They should have also completed the Route Card. Based on the Patrol's hiking experience, you will need to give instruction on why route cards are important, and how they are filled out.

Instructions

- Give out copies of the map with the incident locations marked on. Tell the Patrol that they will be going clockwise/anti-clockwise.

- Allow the Patrol time to work together to complete the plan (10 minutes).

- Check over their plan and approve it. Give pointers if they have made any mistakes.

Notes

It is worth mentioning that the hike being attempted next week is relatively simple. However for longer, more complicated routes, a route plan is an essential part of preparing for the hike, as you can estimate how long it will take you and where you will need to camp if the hike requires an overnight stay.

Resources: Scout Skills factsheet *Route Planning for Hikes* (FS 315083) has more useful information on teaching this skill.

Closing prayer/reflection

'One ought, every day at least, to hear a little song, read a good poem, see a fine picture, and if it were possible, to speak a few reasonable words.' Johann Wolfgang von Goethe, German poet

Thank you God, for the gift of music and the joy of dance. Help us to sing and dance our way through life, and bring joy to others through our singing and dancing. We pray particularly for the residents of the old people's home, that they would enjoy our concert this weekend and that we would do our best to make them smile and sing along.

Amen

WEEK 7B – CONCERT AT OLD PEOPLE'S HOME

This is the culmination of your Troop's song and dance practice. It is also a continuation of your community service; a community event such as this concert will help your Scouts build a practical understanding of both doing their best and helping other people. As well as the performance, there is the opportunity to serve drinks, chat to the residents and listen to their stories. You may discover that one of the Scouts is related to a resident, or that residents were members of Scouting in their youth!

You will need

- Keyboard
- CD player
- One Day Activity Form
- Games equipment
- Cakes/biscuits for residents

Programme Zones:	Community, Creative Expression, Beliefs and Attitudes
Methods:	Design and creativity, Service
Links to badges:	Community Challenge, Creative Challenge, Entertainer Activity Badge
Preparation time:	Prior contact with old people's home, set up instruments and dance space Total 10 minutes
Location:	Local old people's home

Timetable (NB: This sample programme assumes the concert is taking place on a Saturday afternoon – other times may be more appropriate for your Troop/local residential centre)

Time	Activity	Additional Information	Run by
12:00	Meet at normal Meeting Place	Young Leaders can run a game while Scouts arrive.	
12:15	Leave for old people's home		
12:30	Arrive and set up	Residents lunch hour is 12:00 – 12:45	
13:00	Concert begins	Dance is after second song.	
13:45	Serve drinks and cakes to residents.		
14:15	Say goodbyes and leave for Meeting Place.		
14:30	Parents collect Scouts.		

ACTIVITY DETAILS

- Depending on how your rehearsal went at the last Troop meeting, you may feel an extra rehearsal is needed before making your way to the old people's home. If walking there as a Troop, the singers could have an impromptu practice on the way.

- It may be worth a member of the leadership team going ahead to the venue in advance, to check that there is enough space for the dancers to perform and that everything is in order. The residents will take longer to move than the usual audience!

- After the concert there will be chance for the Scouts to provide a service commitment, to work towards their Community Challenge. This can involve serving drinks and cakes, chatting to the residents, and any other tasks identified by the centre manager. Try and ensure that everyone has a job to do.

- As long as you have the relevant permissions, you can use this event as an opportunity to take lots of photos as a good example of your Scouts helping others in the community. Use these in your Group Newsletter or website, or submit the best ones to a local newspaper or District publication. Remember that action shots are better than posed photographs.

Badge links

This programme almost completes the service element of the Community Challenge. Scouts who have been involved in learning the dance and songs, rehearsed them and then performed at the old people's home will have provided about four hours of service. It is recommended that two further hours are given. You could hold a Troop Forum with the Scouts involved to discuss how this could be achieved, and use their ideas to plan a future programme or event. This programme also completes the 'performing' element of the Creative Challenge.

WEEK 8 – INCIDENT HIKE

Hiking is an important part of the Scout programme. It helps Scouts to be aware of their surroundings, improves fitness, requires some key Scouting Skills (map reading, route planning and navigation). It can also be a good time for Scouts to develop relationships within their Troop or Patrol. Punctuating the hike with incidents can also test their problem solving skills, all of which can be put towards the Creative Challenge.

You will need

Each Patrol carries with them:

- Three half cut drainpipes
- Trangia stove with burner
- Mug
- 500ml measuring jug
- A two metre plank of wood
- First Aid kit
- Notepad and pen
- Some unnecessary items (to act as red herrings)
- Map, map reader and compass
- Route plan (devised at the previous week's programme)
- Torch
- Mobile phone (with Leader contact number programmed in)
- Energy snack food

Programme Zones:	Outdoor and Adventure, Creative Expression, Fit for Life
Methods:	Activities outdoors, Team-building activities
Links to badges:	Creative Challenge, Hikes Away Staged Activity Badge
Preparation time:	Route will need planning and walking before meeting (three hours); bases will need setting up and manning.
Location:	If starting at the Meeting Place, you should endeavour to cover footpaths, a wooded area and a place of worship/public building in your route. If this cannot be covered in your locality, you may need to arrange to meet elsewhere or travel to the area of the hike.

Timetable (dispense with opening ceremony if travelling to hiking area)

Time	Activity	Additional Information	Run by
18:45	Meet at hike starting point	Check equipment of each Patrol before they start off.	
19:00	Patrols A & B set off	A clockwise/B anti-clockwise	
19:25	Patrols C & D set off	C clockwise/D anti-clockwise	
20:40-20:45	Patrols A & B return to Meeting Place	Check answers and start game	
21:05 - 21:10	Patrols C & D return to Meeting Place	They submit answers and join game	
20:45	Game		
21:15	Close meeting		

ACTIVITY DETAILS

Incidents (see map for incident locations)

1 – Make a mug of tea

- The Patrol are given 15 minutes to make a mug of tea with a trangia stove
- The water is in a water container five metres away from where they are to put the stove
- Using the equipment they are carrying with them, the Patrol must transport the water into the mug before commencing (i.e. use the jug and drainpipes to pour the water from container to mug).

This base has a 15 minute time limit. It is important to stick to this to prevent a logjam later in the hike.

2 – First Aid scenario

- The Patrol come across a simulated First Aid scenario, set up by two Leaders. It has to properly assess the accident and provide good Emergency Aid before progressing.

3 – Balance beam

- The Patrol arrives at the base and are instructed to stand on the plank of wood they have been carrying and remain on it while carrying out a series of daft tasks.

- They are not to step off the beam at any time, and must work as a team to support each other through the tasks.

- Tasks could include:

  - Line up on the beam in age order

  - Tallest to shortest

  - Only four feet and three hands touching the beam

  - Perform a song and dance routine without falling off

4 – Lateral thinking problems

- The Patrol arrive at the given point and have 10 minutes to solve two out of three lateral thinking problems given them. These are:

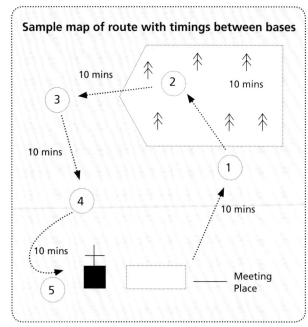

Sample map of route with timings between bases

10 mins · 10 mins · 10 mins · 10 mins · 10 mins · 10 mins

Meeting Place

Problem 1: Starting at 12 noon, and using an analogue clock, how many times in one 12-hour period do the hour and minute hands cross each other?

Answer: 11

(at 12:00, 1:05, 2:10, 3:16, 4:21, 5:27, 6:32, 7:38, 8:43, 9:49 and 10:54)

Problem 2: Two mothers and two daughters go fishing. They only catch three fish, but each of them takes one fish home. How?

Answer: There are three people fishing - a grandmother, her daughter (who is also the mother of), her granddaughter.

Problem 3: I once knew a professional writer, who worked in a cabin. One day, he was sitting in his cabin, writing a letter, when there was a violent thunderstorm, and suddenly he died. How?

Answer: He was a skywriter, and, as he was writing a letter using smoke, in the sky, his plane was hit by lightning, so he died in a plane crash.

5 – Local knowledge

Before returning to the Meeting Place, the Patrol is set the challenge of improving its local knowledge in a way that will require teamwork, observation and concentration. This challenge could be to count the number of windows in a local place of worship or public building; count the number of streetlights between two landmarks; find the date a building was opened by looking for the commemorative plaque – whatever works best for the location of your hike. You will, of course, need to verify the correct answer when planning the activity!

Notes

This activity will require supervision of all the incident bases to run effectively. You can vary the number of incidents based on the adult help available to you, use Young Leaders, or run the hike based on one adult hiking with the Patrol. This adult could also be responsible for supervising each of the incidents in turn when the Patrol arrive at the correct grid reference. This way, you're more likely to stick to time as the adult can offer advice when the Scouts are about to make a wrong turn (although wrong turns are sometimes part of the learning process!)

The route should not be too challenging. Use well defined footpaths, clear route plans (created as part of the programme the week before) and plenty of features to aid navigation. The more important aspect is that the Patrol hikes together carrying their equipment as a team. A route that is too difficult could mean a Patrol gets lost and throws the timings completely out of the window.

It is likely that more than one Patrol may arrive at an incident at the same time (although if timings are strictly observed in the sample route, this will only happen once). This is no problem, as all of the incidents can be attempted by more than one Patrol at once. That is the principle reason for them carrying their own equipment.

Badge links

The lateral thinking problems, balance beam and make a mug of tea incidents can be used to complete the problem solving requirement of the Creative Challenge.

You could easily extend this programme to run at a weekend over a longer time period (with more incidents) and count is as a Hike Away.

Scouting very quickly became a global Movement with its aims, principles and method today stretching to 216 countries and territories. The Global Challenge offers Scouts opportunities to understand that they are part of the worldwide family and to learn about issues that affect people in other parts of the world. This programme, using resources produced by Save the Children, uses a common theme that runs throughout the meeting.

You will need

- Copies of the Free Healthcare Saves Lives poster
- Save the Children resources from POL
- Copies of photo of Prime Minister's face
- Card (cut into long thin strips to make headbands)
- Paper
- Stapler/staples
- Coloured pens/pencils
- Paints
- Scissors

Programme Zone:	Global
Methods:	Themes, Games, Activities with others
Links to badges:	Global Challenge
Preparation time:	
Location:	Indoor – normal Meeting Place

Time	Activity		Additional Information	Run by
19:00	Opening ceremony		Short, leading in to active game	
19:10	Game – Doctor vs Disease			
19:25	Explain game and introduce theme with drama/story		Choose Scouts to read out parts	
19:40	Two Patrols	Two Patrols		
20:00	Prime Minister Dice Game	Free Healthcare Relay Quiz		
	Free Healthcare Relay Quiz	Prime Minister Dice Game		
20:20	Campaign activity			
	Prime Minister message	Headbands message		
20:40	Summary and closing ceremony		Give out notices for overnight and camp cooking next week – refer to Skills Cards for kit list.	

Order from www. scouts.org.uk/shop

ACTIVITY DETAILS

The resources for all the Save the Children activities can be found on www.scouts.org.uk/pol. A colour copy of the poster can be downloaded from the Save the Children website and is also available on Programmes Online.

Doctor vs Disease

This game is a variation on Stuck in the Mud, with a health theme. One Scout is picked to be the Disease. Their aim is to catch as many other Scouts as possible. One other Scout is picked to be the Doctor. They can't be caught by the Disease, as they have been immunised against the Disease. Whenever a Scout is caught, they are infected by the Disease, and have to stand still with their feet shoulder width apart. The Doctor has to cure them from the disease by sliding between their legs.

If these rules are too simplistic for your Troop, use the following suggestions to complicate the game. Extend the game further by playing outdoors and specifying different diseases with different rules…

Infection zone – when a Scout gets caught, the area one metre around them becomes contagious and any Scouts running through it also become infected. They are told so by the Leader, who must use their discretion to judge.

Healthcare is not free – You could make some Scouts citizens of a country where healthcare is not free, e.g. Sierra Leone. When such a Scout is caught, the Doctor has to pick up money from one corner of the room and deposit it in the bank (in the opposite corner) before 'curing' them.

Tips: Choose a reasonably athletic Scout as the Disease. The game should progress in a way in which the Doctor finds it increasingly difficult to cure people of the Disease. Once the game finishes, explain that in some parts of the world, Disease passes much more rapidly between people because they do not have access to the medicine to cure it. On top of this, people have to pay beyond their means for the healthcare that will save lives, and if healthcare was free in these countries a lot more people's lives would be saved.

Introduce the theme

Explain that Save the Children is campaigning for free healthcare for every child in the world, and that this meeting's programme will look at some of the issues that affect people in Africa.

Use the 'Children's stories for you to read' section of the resources to put the meeting in context.

- Ask Scouts to read out the statements as characters, holding photographs of the children they are being.

- A Leader reads out the paragraphs in bold.

- Adapt or shorten the statements but make sure you present a range of experiences.

Prime Minister Dice Game

This is explained in full on the poster on www.scouts.org.uk/pol. Splitting the Troop in half will make the game more manageable.

Free Healthcare Relay Quiz

- Using the 'Quick Q&A' section of the Free Healthcare poster, cut up the questions and the answers and jumble them up, putting them at one end of the Meeting Place.

- Scouts line up in Patrols at the opposite end of the Meeting Place.

- On the word 'go' they race to the end and bring back one piece of paper, tagging the next Scout who continues the relay.

- The winning Patrol is not the one back first, but whichever correctly matches the questions with the answers.

- Go over the answers, so that all the Scouts learn about the issues.

Prime Minister Message

- Scouts split into their Patrols to write a message to the Prime Minister based on what they have heard during the meeting.

- Encourage them to think creatively. Depending on the equipment available to you, they could record a video, send an e-mail, text or dress up as the Prime Minister – whatever comes to mind!

- Make sure that they finish in the time, so that you can send their message to The Prime Minister and Save the Children after the meeting.

Headbands Message

- The other half of the Troop use the 'Stand side-by-side with children in Liberia' activity on the poster to make headbands and decorate them with their messages that they wish to send to the Prime Minister. Have coloured pens, card, paper and paints available for them to get creative.

- Take a photograph of your Scouts, which you can then send to Save the Children at:

Save the Children
1 St John's Lane,
London EC1M 4AR
youthcampaigns@savethechildren.org.uk

Summary

In your closing ceremony, give out copies of the poster for Scouts to display at home. Hold a brief forum with the whole Troop and find out if there is anything else they would like to do about the issues you have discussed. This could include inviting a local councillor or your MP to a Troop meeting, holding a community event to spread the message further, making contact with Scouts in one of the countries you have found out about, etc.

You could finish by reading Patricia and Joyce's Story from the poster, or with a prayer/reflection. You'll also need to brief the Scouts on what they need to bring for next week's meeting, which includes a night away. Use Skills Card 2 – which contains a kit list for camp.

Badge link

This programme meets the 'International Issues' requirement of the Global Challenge.

WEEK 10 – CAMP COOKING CHALLENGE

Cooking outdoors can set a Scout in good stead for life. This programme, which introduces elements of competition and Patrol challenge is a great opportunity for including parents to be part of the meeting, teaming up with Scouts in a supporting role. Scouts will enjoy telling their mums and dads to peel potatoes while the parents will get to see what their children are getting out of Troop life. At the end, you can enjoy the results!

You will need

- Stoves
- Fuel
- Cooking utensils
- Ingredients (access to supermarket)
- Recipe books
- Tents
- Dining shelters
- Matches
- Newspaper (optional)
- Plates, mugs and cutlery
- Tables and chairs
- Lamps
- Ingredients for breakfast
- Nights Away Permit

Programme Zones:	Outdoor and Adventure, Creative Expression
Methods:	Team building activities, Visits and visitors
Links to badges:	Camp Cook Activity Badge
Preparation time:	Book campsite, invite parents, decide on teams, set up campsite in advance
Location:	Campsite/Activity Centre

Timetable (Note the earlier than usual recommended start time)

Time	Activity	Additional Information	Run by
18:00	Meet outside the Troop Meeting Place to travel to a local campsite	Scouts to travel in their Patrols	
18:10	During the journey, reveal details of the Patrol Camp Cooking Challenge		
18:30	Arrive at supermarket. Scouts have 30 minutes to purchase their ingredients.	Need some supervision of Scouts inside supermarket and one Leader at entrance.	
19:00	Continue journey to campsite.		
19:30	Scouts arrive and are given parents to work with in their teams. They must decide on jobs for the adults to do to help them.		
19:45	Cooking time begins.		
20:30-21:00	Dinner is served, after which teams wash up and clear cooking area ready for breakfast.		
21:00	Evening entertainment		
22:30	Lights out		

ACTIVITY DETAILS

This programme will take more advance planning and preparation than any other this term, but is potentially very rewarding. It involves Leaders, young people and parents alike. The main preparation task is to set up the campsite for those taking part before everyone arrives, so that you can get on with the task in hand on the evening of the programme. Of course, you could run the programme at a campsite with indoor accommodation, which will allow you to focus on setting up the outdoor cooking areas for each Patrol, using whatever camp cooking equipment is at your Group's disposal. Use the checklist on the next page to make sure everything is done on time…

Camp Cooking Challenge checklist

○ Book campsite.

○ Arrange transport to campsite.

○ Withdraw cash from Group funds to give Patrol Leader as budget.

○ Send out invitations to parents/carers (with return slip/phone number).

○ Plan route to campsite to include a stop at a supermarket.

○ Confirm supermarket opening hours.

○ Check Troop/Patrol equipment (make any necessary repairs).

○ Confirm with parents who are attending and give them timings of when to arrive (recommend 7pm at campsite so they can pitch their tents with assistance before Scouts arrive).

Day of/before camp:

○ Print out instructions for challenge to give to Patrol Leaders on journey (plus copies for Leaders).

○ Purchase ingredients for breakfast as required.

○ Go to campsite to set up camping/cooking areas.

○ Pitch Patrol tents.

○ Mark out parents'/Leaders' campsite.

○ Pitch your tent.

○ Pitch dining shelters and set up camp kitchens.

○ Return to meeting place to pick up Scouts.

Instructions

- Details of the Camp Cooking Challenge should, as far as possible, be kept secret from the Scouts. You may wish to inform the parents that they will be helping Scouts cook a meal, but to keep it from them.

- Once the journey is underway, written details of the challenge should be given to each Patrol Leader. An example of what to write is given below.

CAMP COOKING CHALLENGE

Tonight, your task is to design a menu, buy the ingredients and cook an evening meal as a Patrol.

You have twenty minutes to decide what you will be cooking and what ingredients you need.

You will then have thirty minutes to buy your ingredients at a supermarket.

You will have the use of a camp kitchen at the campsite with an altar fire and gas stove.

You will have the help of parents, who are joining us for the camp. They are not allowed to take charge – you have to tell them what to do!

Your budget for this menu is £15.

- Give them a selection of recipe books to help them choose what to cook (their own ideas may be better). Listen to the discussions and make sure their plans include at least two courses, or a large main meal.

- If the Patrols are travelling separately, e.g. in cars, you will need other adults to give out the instructions and supervise the discussion.

- At the supermarket, have a few adults wandering around the shop to advise the Scouts should they need it. One Leader should remain at the front entrance ensuring all the Scouts are counted in and out of the shop so you don't leave anyone behind.

- When you arrive at the campsite, assign parents to each of the teams, and explain to them that their role is not to take charge but to follow orders! They might be able to help with fire lighting and feeding the fire (if you are using wood fires).

- It may be helpful to have a central store of basic ingredients, e.g. cooking oil, seasoning, sauces, flour, milk, should anyone have accidentally forgotten something or run out. You will also need to provide breakfast in the morning, so these can be stored together.

- The Patrols have 45-75 minutes to prepare and eat their meals. Be flexible with this time as cooking/preparation times will vary, and it's more important that the Scouts enjoy their meal than rush and ruin it.

- To continue the competitive element, someone should judge the meals using a list of criteria, e.g. flavour, balanced diet, presentation, originality, etc. You could invite a special guest to do the judging.

- Announce the winners, thank everyone for taking part, clean up and then finish the evening with some entertainment, such as a campfire. All that's left to do is have a good night's sleep and cook breakfast, before continuing your camp or heading home.

Notes

- This programme assumes that Scouts in the Troop have a knowledge and experience of fire-lighting and cooking at camp. If running a new or less experienced Troop, it is recommended that you cover fire lighting and basic camp cooking earlier in the term's programme.
- Factsheets on *Fire Lighting* (FS 315076) and *Basic Cooking* (FS 315075) may be useful resources for this programme.

Resources

Sample letter of invitation to parents

⌐SCOUTS⌐

Dear Parent,

In a few weeks time on Friday 14 April, the Troop will be going to Fairweather Campsite for an inter-Patrol Camp Cooking Challenge. This is an overnight event to which parents are invited to join the Scouts camping.

The challenge will involve planning a menu, buying the ingredients at a supermarket and then cooking it outdoors at the campsite. Parents will be assigned to Scout teams, and it is usual for them to follow the orders of the Scouts!

Please can you let me know whether you're available to attend. We will meet at the Troop Meeting Place at 6.30pm and congregate at the campsite at 7.30pm. If you require a tent, please let me know. If bringing your own, I recommend you arrive at the campsite at 7.00pm to pitch it in the adults camping area.

I look forward to dining with you on the 14th!

Hugh

07123 456 789/hugh.leader@email.co.uk

Badge links

This programme will provide first time campers with a Nights Away Badge, and could count towards requirement 1 of the Camp Cook Activity Badge.

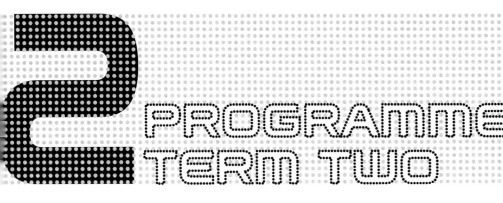

PROGRAMME PLAN TERM TWO

THIS TERM COVERS ALL THE ZONES AND WORK TOWARDS FIVE OF THE CHALLENGES, COMPLETING THE COMMUNITY CHALLENGE AND THE FITNESS CHALLENGE.

Scouting skills covered include shelter building, emergency aid, pioneering and hiking. You will spend at least one Night Away and complete one Hike Away. Three of the programmes involve visits or visitors and you will need to arrange extra adult help on three occasions. This term you will link with the Explorer Scout Section and invite parents to help with the bake-a-thon. You might meet away from the Meeting Place in weeks seven and 10. An unusual item you may need to purchase in advance is a parachute!

Week	Programme	Zone	Methods
1	Fitness Challenge 1	F	G
2	Charity bake-a-thon	CE / F	DC
2b	Cake sale	C	S
3	Shelter building	OA / F	AO / TBA
4	Looking after each other	BA / F / OA	S / AwO / TBA
5	Reduce/reuse/recycle	G / C / F	VV / PWR / T
6	Recycling scavenger hunt	C / G / OA	S / AO / TBA / T
7	Splash!	F / OA	AO / TBA
8	Pioneering project	OA / CE	AO / AwO
9	Games night - led by Patrol Leaders or Explorer Section	F / OA	G / VV
10	Jamboree-on-the-Trail	G / OA / F	AO / AwO / VV

BADGES WORKED TOWARDS THIS TERM

PROGRAMME METHODS

SCOUTS

PROGRAMME ZONES	Activities Outdoors	Games	Design & creativity	Visits & visitors	Service	Technology & new skills	Team building activities	Activities with others	Themes	Prayer worship & reflection
Outdoor & Adventure	✓	✓ ✓					✓	✓ ✓		
Global	✓			✓ ✓			✓			
Community				✓ ✓	✓		✓			
Fit for Life	✓	✓ ✓		✓					✓	
Creative Expression			✓					✓		
Beliefs & Attitudes					✓			✓		✓

The Bottom Line

Activity	Fun	Teamwork	Leadership	Relationships	Commitment	Personal development
○○○	○○○	○○○	○○○	○○○	○○○	○○○

1 tick = Poor
2 ticks = Good
3 ticks = Excellent

CONTACTS FOR THIS TERM'S PROGRAMME

District/County Leaders' Meeting –
Ask about survival skills at meeting.

District Commissioner –
Activity approval.

Water Activity Provider –
(e.g. ACC Activities, sailing instructor) – book activities, arrange dates.

Explorer Scout Leader –
Organise week nine.

JOTT UK Coordinator –
register for Jamboree-on-the-Trail (JOTT).

International Links –
Find overseas contact for JOTT.

Scout Troop in another country –
Make contact before JOTT and arrange activity.

CHECKLIST FOR TERM'S PROGRAMME:

1. Book campsite activities for term.
2. Book external providers.
3. Arrange date for Recycling Officer visit.
4. Invite parents to Fitness Challenge presentation.
5. Write parent letter detailing weekend commitments (Cake Sale, JOTT).
6. Re-stock First Aid Kit.
7. Arrange extra adult help for programmes 2, 6 and 10.
8. Order badges from Badge Secretary.

WEEK 1 – FITNESS CHALLENGE 1

There are two ways to approach The Fitness Challenge: you can prepare your Scouts for a special event, such as a charity swim, and spend over four weeks training for it. Alternatively, the Troop can work together to develop a particular physical activity, through activities like circuit training or aerobics. In this programme, which stretches until week five, the second route is taken, and the whole Troop involved in the training. Your Troop may have specific individual needs, so that you will need to adapt the content of the training programme. However the principles of these plans will provide you with the framework for successfully completing the challenge.

You will need

- Mats
- Stopwatch
- Box for box jumps
- Thick rope (5m long)
- Weight to attach to rope
- Cones/markers
- Water/cups
- Record cards
- Pencils/pens

Programme Zone:	Fit for Life
Method:	Games
Links to badges:	Fitness Challenge
Preparation time:	Meeting place needs adapting for fitness exercises (mats, etc) and Troop need time to change into activity wear. Make simple record cards and copy for each Scout.
Location:	Indoor and possibly outdoor

Timetable

Time	Activity		Additional Information	Run by
19:00	Opening Ceremony			
19:15	Game – Chairball		See page 84	
19:30	Fitness Challenge – the lowdown		Explain the challenge and choices. Demonstrate exercises for circuits. • Sit ups • Squat thrusts • Box jumps • Rope exercise • Shuttle runs	
19:45	Juice break			
19:50	Warm-up		Include stretching and breathing exercises.	
20:00	Trial runs			
	Half Troop	Half Troop		
	Circuits	Aerobics		
20:15	Aerobics	Circuits		
20:30	Warm down all together.			
20:40	Fill out Record Cards.			
20:50	Closing Ceremony			

In more detail

In explaining the Challenge to the Troop, you may wish to refer them to the requirements as printed in the *Scout Record Book* or *Scout Badge Book*. Explain that the things you will be looking for are commitment and a demonstration of improvement over the four weeks.

The circuit activities will need to be set up in one half of the Meeting Place (and possibly outside it as well) – the aerobics will occupy the other half of the Meeting Place.

Tell the Scouts that they will have a go at both physical activities in this meeting, and then get to decide which they would like to practise for their Fitness Challenge.

Sit ups – There are many ways to do these, but for doing lots over a two minute period, the best is to go from a flat lying position with hands resting on thighs, sitting up sliding the hands to the knees and repeat.

Squat thrusts – Start in press-up position and jump both feet up to land in between hands, which do not move. Jump back to start position. This counts as one. Repeat, ensuring that the body continues to be fully extended.

Box jumps – From a standing position jump on to a box (about chest height) and jump down the other side. This counts as one. Jump back to the starting position. Repeat, doing as many as possible in two minutes.

Rope exercise – If you have the facilities, Scouts can climb up a rope (or a rope ladder) and ring a bell at the top. Return to the bottom of the rope. Repeat, doing as many as possible in two minutes. Alternatively, attach a weight to a 5m rope. The exercise is to pull the weight to yourself, then run 5m to stretch out the rope. Repeat, doing as many as possible in two minutes.

Shuttle runs – mark out two cones five metres apart. Simply, Scouts run between the two markers. Running from A to B and back again counts as one. Do as many shuttles in two minutes.

Instructions

- Scouts have two minutes to attempt each exercise.

- One minute of rest is timed in between for Scouts to move between exercises and have a drink/breather.

Notes

The first circuit round, expect Scouts to burn out in the first minute and struggle to sustain exercise until the end of the two minutes. This is okay, but have plenty of water on hand and be prepared to increase the rest minutes. This is one of the aspects of the challenge that the Scouts will be able to improve over the weeks of practice.

- After the trials, you will need to get each of the Scouts to fill out a Record Card for their practice. This could include recording the pulse rate before and after the aerobics session, and recording the total sit ups, etc. performed in the two minute period of activity.

- Explain that these Record Cards will need to be filled in after each session in the next few weeks to use as evidence for awarding the Fitness Challenge.

- Allow sufficient time for warm up and warm down (these should be included in your Risk Assessment of the programme).

Note

The person leading your aerobics session may be a parent, or a local fitness instructor who runs an aerobics class. If they are not available for the duration of the Challenge, you will need to find someone who is able to 'lead' the routine in subsequent weeks. This could be a member of the Troop or a member of your leadership team.

Sample layout of Meeting Place for Fitness Challenge

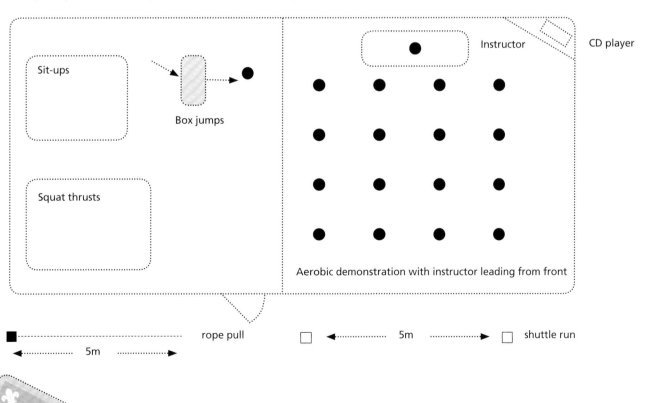

Badge link

This programme goes towards the Fitness Challenge, to be completed over subsequent weeks.

WEEK 2 - CHARITY BAKE-A-THON

If you followed the programme in term one to perform a concert for a local old people's home, you will still need to provide a few hours community service to complete the Community Challenge. This programme can count towards that, but provides a creative element also, as the Troop work together to bake as many cakes as possible to sell at a community event that supports the centre you worked with last term. There is also the chance to involve parents and/or Group supporters in the life of the Troop, as you will need people on hand to support your bake-a-thon.

Note: This programme divides the Troop by the activity they have chosen for the Fitness Challenge.

You will need

- Cake tins (at least two)
- Baking cases (100)
- Whisks
- Wooden spoons
- Skewers
- Cooling racks
- Paper plates
- Cling-film/labels

For each batch of 24 mini cakes:

- 125g unsalted butter, softened
- 125g caster sugar
- 2 large eggs
- 125g self-raising flour
- 1 tsp vanilla extract
- 2-3 tbsp milk
- 500g pack instant icing (or other toppings as decided by Scouts)
- Washing up equipment
- Tables

Programme Zones:	Creative Expression, Fit for Life
Method:	Design and creativity
Links to badges:	Fitness Challenge, Community Challenge, Chef Activity Badge (req. 3), Nights Away Staged Activity Badge
Preparation time:	Shopping for ingredients/requires extra adult help
Location:	Indoor at location with fully fitted kitchen /sleeping accommodation

Timetable

Time	Activity				Additional Information	Run by
19:00	Opening ceremony					
19:10	Aerobics 1	Aerobics 2	Circuits 1	Circuits 2		
	Kitchen	Preparation 1	Preparation 2	Circuits		
19:30	Preparation 1	Preparation 2	Circuits	Kitchen		
19:50	Preparation 2	Kitchen	Washing Up	Preparation 1		
20:10	Aerobics	Aerobics	Preparation 1	Preparation 2		
20:30	Washing up	Washing up	Kitchen	Washing up		
20:50	Packaging	Toppings	Packaging	Toppings		

ACTIVITY DETAILS

- The above timetable assumes four groupings, each half the size of the groups practicing for the Fitness Challenge. Adjust the groupings and sizes (to accommodate more than four if necessary) depending on the size of the Troop and the take-up of the Fitness Challenge. Groupings can be as small as four Scouts for the production chain.

- The aim of this programme is to bake as many cakes as possible in a designated time period. To add an element of fun and adventure, you could combine this task with a sleepover, using a building with a kitchen.

- The simplest way to hold your bake-a-thon is to set up a production line, where different parts of the process get done in pieces. We have broken down the process as follows, but you may have a different, equally efficient way of organising things.

- You will need to give thought to how the Scouts get dressed/cleaned up after their physical exercise; it's good to have adults responsible for each base in case timings slip a little!

Preparation 1
- Mix butter with sugar
- Add egg/vanilla extract
- Sift in flour

Team changes to toppings once all cakes have cooled.

Preparation 2
- Prepare tins
- Add milk
- Spoon into tin

Team changes to toppings once cakes have cooled.

Kitchen
- Pre-heat oven
- Bake for 12 minutes
- Cool for 5 minutes
- Empty tin

Washing up
- Wash/rinse used tins
- Wash utensils
- Return to correct place

Change to packaging once cakes have cooled.

Sample recipe

This tried and tested recipe is for simple fairy cakes. However varying the style and flavour of cakes can increase the challenge. Perhaps the Patrols could each come with a different recipe to try. Remember, each time you change the recipe, the people on the production lines will need to be informed!

Fairy cakes

Use the ingredients listed above and follow these instructions:

- Preheat the ovens to 190°C/375F/Gas mark 5.
- Place paper cases in the holes of the baking tin.
- In a mixing bowl beat the butter and sugar until pale and fluffy using a whisk or wooden spoon.
- Add the beaten egg, a little at a time, whisking to incorporate, then beat in the vanilla.
- Fold half of the flour into the mixture.
- Add the milk and the rest of the flour. Fold until well combined.
- Spoon into the tin and bake for 12 minutes (or until risen and golden on top).
- Allow to cool for 5-10 minutes on a rack before removing from the tin.
- Top with icing or another topping as desired!

Notes

- You can repeat the rotation (but only do the fitness exercise once) until you have exhausted your ingredients. Combining the bake-a-thon with a sleepover has its advantages, as it will means you will have more time, and able to achieve more than under usual meeting conditions.
- Involving parents in the meeting can be a good way of introducing them to Troop life, as this programme scores highly on many 'bottom line' aspects: activity; fun; teamwork; relationships (as well as opportunities for leadership of various production areas, and commitment, depending on how long you continue the chain!).
- You will need constant supervision of the kitchen, and someone overseeing the mixing of ingredients. By setting up the preparation areas in the main meeting space (i.e. out of the kitchen) on tables, and putting an adult on each of these bases, the production process can be controlled.

- Remember that as a small group comes to a base for the first time, they will need a brief explanation/demonstration of what they need to do there! As time goes on, you will need to take less and less a leadership role.
- Make sure there is enough cool storage space for the cakes, as you will be selling these at a later date and need to ensure they are preserved well. Once all the cakes are cooled, two small groups can be responsible for topping them and two groups can carry out the packaging, covering a selection of cakes with cling film and sticking price labels on them.
- By installing someone as 'quality control,' some reject cakes can be withdrawn and eaten by the Scouts by way of a reward!
- Depending on the amount of ingredients you bring in, this programme could occupy the whole night. You may however, prefer to finish at a reasonable time and play games or make use of other facilities your sleepover venue has to offer.

Badge links

This programme links to many badges, but can provide up to four hours community service needed to complete the Community Challenge Area 2.

WEEK 2B – CAKE SALE (WEEKEND EVENT)

CAKES FOR SALE!

As the final part of your Community Challenge service project, a cake sale at a local event to raise money for the old people's home visited in term 1 will link your community visit to this term's creative cookery. You will probably need to hold the cake sale at a weekend, so the commitment from the Troop will need to be advertised well in advance. The cake sale is a good chance to show members of the local community that Scouts help others and support local causes. It is also an opportunity to advertise for new Members, so take along leaflets and be prepared to take down details of anyone interested in joining.

You will need

- Cakes made at previous meeting
- Tables to sell from
- Small change float
- Smart uniform
- One day activity form (if far from usual Meeting Place)
- Promotional leaflets/banners
- CD Player with aerobics track

Programme Zone:	Community
Method:	Service
Links to badges:	Community Challenge
Preparation time:	Arrive one hour early to set up cake stall and arrange float
Location:	Local community event, e.g. school/village fair.

Timetable

Time	Activity	Additional Information	Run by
11:00	Set up your stall, bringing all the cakes made at the previous meeting.		
12:00	The event begins. As Scouts arrive to help, check uniform and explain how stall works		
16:00	Event finishes. Pack up, thank organisers, go home, count money.		

ACTIVITY DETAILS

- Compared to the rigorous events of the previous meeting, this programme is relatively simple to run.

- It will be helpful if you ask the Scouts to arrive in small groups on a rota basis, so that the stall does not appear overrun by helpers. The simplest way to do this is in Patrols; each can be given an hour to go round the rest of the event together and spend their pocket money.

- When Scouts arrive to help, make sure they each have a job to do. Some can be handing out flyers and talking about Scouting; some can be selling cakes; some can be handling the money; some can be keeping your area clean and tidy.

- As this programme coincides with your Troop practicing the Fitness Challenge, you may be able to arrange for the Troop to demonstrate their aerobics routine, with others able to join in if they pay a small fee. All the money goes to the old people's home, so this is an easy way to cash in on people's good will!

- Once the event is over and you have counted the money, contact the old people's home to let them know how much you have raised. You could arrange to present a cheque at the centre with some of the Scouts present. Alternatively, you could revisit the home with some Troop members to say hello to the residents and give in the money.

Badge link

This programme completes the Community Service aspect of the Community Challenge. Those Scouts that have been continuously involved in the activities (concert, bake-a-thon and cake sale) can now be awarded the Challenge Badge.

WEEK 3 - SHELTER BUILDING

Survival skills are perhaps less relevant today, with the wide range of hi-tech lightweight tents that Scouts are able to carry with them on expeditions. However, there are few Scouts who don't enjoy learning survival techniques. The popularity of adventurers like Ray Mears and Bear Grylls testifies to the interest survival still holds. Building a shelter could be the start of a lifelong passion for survival training, and is a good introduction to the Survival Skills Activity Badge.

You will need

- Groundsheets
- Dead wood
- Vegetation (leaves, bracken, etc.)
- Sisal, twine, etc.
- Axe/saw
- Step ladder
- Scouts should wear boots/outdoor clothing
- Parachute (old)
- Tent pegs

Useful resources

- *SAS Survival Handbook*, John 'Lofty Wiseman', Collins, 2003.
- *Camping, Hiking and Wilderness Skills*, Peter G. Drake, Lorenz Books, 2004

Programme Zones:	Outdoor and adventure, Fit for life
Methods:	Activities outdoors, Team building activities, Prayer, worship and reflection
Links to badges:	Fitness Challenge, Survival Skills Activity Badge
Preparation time:	If setting up sample shelters before meeting, you will need to arrive 90 minutes earlier than usual. Set up meeting place for Fitness Challenge – 10 minutes.
Location:	Outdoor location with access to materials to make shelters from (Scout campsite or woodland is ideal)

Time	Activity	Additional Information	Run by
19:00	Opening Ceremony		
19:15	Types of shelter		
19:35	Fitness Challenge		
20:00	Shelter building (in Patrols) • Bough shelter • Bivouac • Groundsheet shelter		
20:55	Outdoor Closing Ceremony		

ACTIVITY DETAILS

- If you are not accustomed to teaching survival skills, you may like to invite someone more experienced in this area to lead the session. Ask at a County or District Leaders' meeting, or ask your ADC/ACC Scouts or equivalent.

- Introduce the topic of survival by talking about why you may need to build a shelter; the different types of shelter and the importance of looking around you to make use of natural resources. Some of these details are covered on the next page.

- Ask questions and get the Scouts to discuss the answers given by their peers, so that it's not just you talking.

- You may wish to set up some examples of shelters before the meeting, so that the Scouts can have a look and test them out before attempting to build their own. Of course, be careful to leave some materials for the Scouts to build their shelters!

- Use some Native American verses (see below), which celebrate and respect the Earth. This will set the activity within a more reflective context. Once the Scouts have built their shelters, it could be a chance for them to spend some time in silence, listening to the sounds of nature and reflecting on how people rely on the Earth to sustain them. What ways do we rely on natural resources? How can we be more responsible through our daily actions? What change would we like to make in our world?

Treat the earth well.
It was not given to you by your parents,
it was loaned to you by your children.
We do not inherit the Earth from our Ancestors,
we borrow it from our Children.
Ancient Indian Proverb

I do not think the measure of a civilization is how tall its buildings of concrete are, but rather how well its people have learned to relate to their environment and fellow man.

Sun Bear of the Chippewa Tribe

Types of shelter

Bivouac

Show the stages of building one from scratch, and how important square lashings are to their construction.

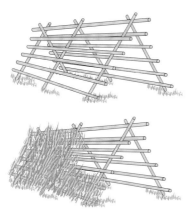

Lean-to shelter

Making use of walls or trees, the lean-to can take some of the work out of the construction, and provide natural shelter. Stress the importance of building your shelter on the leeward side of the tree/wall.

Bough shelter

This shelter may be hard to demonstrate, as it makes use of fallen trees. If you're lucky enough to find one, then it is worth showing. Reinforce the bough by lashing to the base of another branch where it forks from the tree.

Tipis

Probably best known in its North American cultural context, the tipi can actually be found in cultures across the world. As a survival shelter, you only need to make the tepee big enough for you to sleep in.

- Make your cone shape from three or more angled supports, and tie together where they cross.

- Cover with parachute material or plastic sheeting, and fix at the base. Leave an opening at the top for ventilation.

Groundsheet shelters

These are quick and easy, and can make use of any waterproof material, including a jackets. Use string or wood as the ridge, and make use of standing trees. Find bracken and/or dry grass to use as bedding. Use multiple layers for extra waterproofing.

Notes

To hold your normal closing ceremony outdoors, construct a flagpole while the Scouts are building their shelters. This could be completed by Young Leaders or Scouts who are familiar with shelter-building as an extra challenge.

Badge links

Extend this programme to include a Night Away and you will complete the bivouac element of the Outdoor Plus Challenge.

This programme could also count towards the Survival Skills Activity Badge. Scouts who show a keen interest in the activity may benefit from a Survival Skills course, which could be organised at Group, District or County level.

WEEK 4 – LOOKING AFTER EACH OTHER

Troop Forums are an important part of running a healthy Troop. They enable every member of the Troop to have their say and can be an invaluable way of coming up with ideas for popular future programmes. One responsibility of the Troop Forum is to draw up and maintain the Troop Code of Conduct. This programme lays out a possible process for doing this.

You will need

- First Aid Kit
- Equipment for First Aid scenarios
- CD Player for aerobics
- Kit for Fitness Challenge

Programme Zone(s):	Beliefs and Attitudes, Fit for Life, Community
Method:	Games
Links to badges:	Emergency Aid Staged Badges
Preparation time:	10 minutes to set up First Aid scenarios (during coming-in game); normal set up time for Fitness Challenges.
Location:	Indoor – normal Meeting Place

Timetable

Time	Activity	Additional Information	Run by
Before meeting	Trust games	Coming-in game Needs supervision In pairs	
19:00	Opening ceremony	Explain that there will be various things going on at the meeting, and that you want to see a real improvement in their performance for the Fitness Challenge.	
19:20	Emergency Aid	To cover: • burns and scalds • cleaning and dressing wounds • bleeding.	
19:55	Game – cat and mouse	See page 83	
20:00	Troop Forum – Troop Code of Conduct	Patrol Leader to chair the Forum as part of their Promise Challenge.	
20:30	Fitness Challenge	In usual two groups	
20:55	Closing ceremony		

ACTIVITY DETAILS

Trust games

These can be useful exercises to build trust and teamwork within the Troop, particularly when you are experiencing challenging behaviour among members. Though the activities themselves may seem simple, the fundamental principles underlying them can improve the trust between Scouts. For some young people this can be the most difficult thing to give another person.

- In pairs, Scouts stand one in front of the other, facing the same direction.

- The Scout in front closes their eyes and, keeping their body straight, leans back, falling towards the other.

- The Scout behind places both hands behind the shoulders, stopping the other Scout falling, and gently pushing them back to a standing position.

- Repeat, increasing the 'trust' distance.

- Swap positions, repeating the exercise.

When more Scouts have arrived, gather them in two lines with a table in between. One Scout stands on the table, facing away from the rest of the Scouts, and falls backwards, being caught by their friends. This exercise needs a little more coordination so that you're sure everyone is concentrating.

Emergency Aid

Set up a combination of instruction sessions and scenarios to teach and test appropriate aspects of the Staged Emergency Aid Activity Badge. New Scouts that haven't encountered any First Aid before will need to start with the basics, but some Scouts may already have earned an Emergency Aid Staged Badge. However, Emergency Aid should be revisited regularly to reinforce training and to refresh the memory. Scenarios are the most realistic way of applying what you have learnt, but these will not get across all the learning, as there is always one person in a group that takes the lead.

You may find the resources for the Emergency Aid Staged Badge requirements on Programmes Online useful. These cover all the requirements for stages 1-3.

- Assess what level your Scouts are at, so that you know how many bases to offer.

- Find adults/instructors who can provide 10 minute training sessions on the areas of First Aid you are aiming to cover

- Create scenarios (either written or role play) that you can use to test the Scouts at the end of the session. This is best attempted in small groups/Patrols.

Troop Forum

- A well established Troop Forum will essentially run itself with Scouts taking the lead in discussions and deciding who speaks when. If it is the first time you are attempting a Troop Forum, you may need to take more of a lead until ground rules are established.

- Plan something exciting directly after the Troop Forum, so that the Scouts have an incentive to conclude the items you need to discuss.

- The purpose of this Troop Forum is to agree or draw up a Code of Conduct that all members of the Troop must follow. It is important that everyone has a chance to put their ideas across, and that no-one's idea is rejected without being considered. One way of doing this is by having an item (e.g. a piece of wood or woggle) that is passed around in turn. Everyone has a chance to say something when the item comes to them. If they don't have anything to say, they can pass it on. This also has the advantage of silencing the 'loud mouths' in the Troop!

- Don't have too many points to your Code of Conduct so that it is too hard to remember and follow. Once you've got the ideas together, narrow it down to up to 10 good ones. You could use a vote or the clap-o-meter method to decide upon these. Once they're agreed, write them out neatly (or type them up) so that the whole Troop can sign their names underneath.

- Display the code in your Meeting Place until you're ready to review it and agree them again.

- A sample Code of Conduct is opposite page, but rather than using this as a starting point, allow the Scouts to give their ideas and use it as an aid to discussion if necessary...

Our Code of Conduct

At all times we should:

Listen and follow the instructions given by our Leaders, Patrol Leaders and Assistant Patrol Leaders.

Turn up on time, so we can start and finish on time, and be prepared to join in.

Be intolerant of bullying, swearing and not do it ourselves!

Wear sensible clothes and footwear for the activities we're doing.

Be honest and say what we think, feel, want or need, provided it is at an appropriate time and not hurtful towards others.

Set a good example to younger Scouts or Cubs.

Remember to say please and thank you, and most importantly, smile and have fun!

During meetings we should:

- Turn our mobile phones off or keep them silent.
- Put sweets or chewing gum away, so we're not tempted to eat them.
- Turn up in smart uniform, unless we're told otherwise by a Leader.

Above all we should:

- Show loyalty to our Troop and the worldwide Movement.
- Be able to be trusted and trust others.
- Be a considerate friend to others.
- Be brave, even when the going is tough.
- Be careful with other people's stuff as well as our own.
- Treat each other with respect.

Badge links

Fitness Challenge (nearly finished!), Promise Challenge (requirements 'i' and 'j'), Emergency Aid Staged Badges.

WEEK 5 – REDUCE, REUSE, RECYCLE

You can't go anywhere these days without seeing an advert for recycling, recycling bins or the two arrows telling us that our food packaging can be recycled. But how much do your Scouts know about recycling and why it is important? Spend a meeting finding out, by inviting a Recycling Officer from your local authority to come and talk to the Troop. (This meeting also sees the end of the Fitness Challenge).

You will need

- Equipment required by visitor (tables laid out, etc.)
- CD player
- Equipment for circuits
- Fitness Challenge Badges
- Chairs for parents

Programme Zones:	Global, Community
Method:	Visits and visitors
Links to badges:	Global Conservation Activity Badge
Preparation time:	Arrange visit from local Recycling Officer beforehand. Set out Meeting Place as requested.
Location:	Indoor – normal Meeting Place

Timetable

Time	Activity	Additional Information	Run by
19:00	Opening Ceremony	Use 3 Rs in reflection (see notes)	
19:10	Recycling Workshop	Visit from local council Recycling Officer	
20:05	Warm-up for Fitness Challenges	Parents arrive and are seated	
20:10	Aerobics workout		
20:30	Circuits workout		
20:50	Badge presentation and flag down		

ACTIVITY DETAILS

Opening Ceremony

In your opening ceremony, introduce the theme of recycling through a reflection based on the '3 Rs' of reduce, reuse and recycle...

Reduce – use a really quiet voice to say a prayer or reflection or to talk about recycling.

Reuse – use a popular prayer or song that all the Scouts have heard before

Recycle – say a sentence, which the Scouts repeat back at you, recycling it.

Recycling workshop

Almost all local authorities have Recycling Officers whose job it is to promote recycling and environmental matters to young people. Often they are looking for opportunities to talk to young people about what they can do to conserve the Earth's resources, and will be only too happy to come to your meeting and run a workshop.

Use the local services directory at www.direct.gov.uk or your phone book to contact your local council, and ask to speak to the Recycling Officer responsible for children and youth. Arrange a time for them to come to your Meeting Place, and discuss with them the kind of activities they can provide and what equipment you will need to bring for them.

If they need guidance, it would be good to include some sort of game based around recycling, an active discussion, a recycling activity and an action or campaign that they could start planning based on recycling. This could be a letter/video message to an MP, a poster for the public to promote recycling services, etc.

Alternatively, the Troop could visit the local recycling centre to meet with a Recycling Officer. He or she could explain what happens when recyclable materials arrive there and what they can do at home to help the process run more smoothly.

Badge requirement met by programme

Extending this activity, you could meet all the requirements of the Global Conservation Activity Badge. The main point of this badge is to 'think global, act local.' However it is a good idea to look at the global effect of poor waste management, climate change, etc. A range of climate change activities are available online at www.scouts.org.uk/climatechange

Global Conservation Activity Badge

Complete the requirements below:

1. Find out about an environmental issue that is important to your local community. Examples include:

- recycling
- energy efficiency in the home
- water conservation
- local conservation groups
- water or air pollution

2. Take part in a Troop activity that improves local conservation. Examples include:

- recycling
- wildlife
- energy
- pollution
- traffic fumes

The activity should involve at least five sessions over some weeks or a more concentrated project done over a shorter period of time, perhaps at a weekend conservation camp.

3. Get involved in a campaign to make others aware of an environmental issue. Examples might include:

- Writing about it to your MP or other local agencies
- Use of an original, eye-catching method to inform others about saving energy or resources
- Speaking to a community group
- Recycling printer cartridges, tools or spectacles etc to aid an overseas development project.

Fitness Challenge:

- When the Troop shows commitment and has worked hard at something over a period of time, it is good to acknowledge that in front of an audience.

- Consider inviting parents into the end of the meeting so that they can watch the two Fitness Challenge groups do their last exercise routine.

- By now, the performance should be showing a definite improvement from the first time they tried the exercises. The circuit group will be able to do more than ever in the time, and the aerobic routine will feel easier to complete.

- When the two groups have completed their activities and filled out their Record Cards, ask them to get into uniform and form a circle or horseshoe, with the parents behind this.

Say a few words about the way the Troop has worked hard on this for a number of weeks and thoroughly deserve their Fitness Challenges - one of eight Challenges needed to attain the Chief Scout's Gold Award. It could be an appropriate time to say that it is good to see so many parents supporting their children and that help is always appreciated during the meeting and to talk to you afterwards if they would like to be more involved.

- Present the Challenges in whatever way is your custom.

- Finish the meeting with flag down.

Badge link

After five weeks of practice, the Fitness Challenge is complete.

WEEK 6 - RECYCLING SCAVENGER HUNT

A scavenger hunt is an enduringly popular way of running a Scout meeting. It adds a sense of adventure and independence to an activity by sending Scouts outside the Meeting Place to achieve a series of tasks. The Scouts will need to be in small groups of equal ability and experience so that no one is left out of their depth. This scavenger hunt extends the theme of recycling from the previous meeting and if nothing else will leave the community a little cleaner than you found it.

You will need

- Gloves (each Scout to bring)
- Maps of local area
- Compass (per Patrol)
- Notepads and pens
- Digital cameras/phones
- Bags to collect items in

Programme Zones:	Outdoor and Adventure, Global, Community
Methods:	Themes, Games, Team-building activities, Service
Links to badges:	Global Conservation Activity Badge
Preparation time:	To adapt the scavenger hunt list, you may need to make a tour of the local area to ensure all the information is accurate and that the task is feasible in the time allowed.
Location:	Meet at normal Meeting Place; scavenger hunt happens in local area.

Timetable

Time	Activity	Additional Information	Run by
19:00	Opening Ceremony		
19:10	Break into teams/Patrols of equal number. Give out scavenger hunt lists.	All Scouts to wear gloves	
19:15	Scavenger hunt starts		
20:30	Deadline to return to Meeting Place. Play game while waiting for all to return and while adding up scores.		
20:50	Announce winner and closing ceremony.		

ACTIVITY DETAILS

- The purpose of this activity is to get the Scouts working well as part of a team. It will also help them discover their local recycling point, what can and can't be recycled, as well as the importance of making use of time.

- Write a list of tasks to do in the local area around the theme of recycling. A conventional scavenger hunt will involve finding things lying around, but could incorporate stopping people to ask them the answer to a question, or 'collecting' things such as songs, photographs and stories.

- Before the meeting, find all the recycling points in the area local to your Meeting Place. These may involve:

  - bottle banks
  - charity shops (for clothes and furniture)
  - supermarkets
  - paper recycling bins
  - recycling centres
  - door-to-door bag/box collections.

- Assuming some or all of these are within walking distance of the Meeting Place, build the tasks on the list around getting to as many of these in the time set.

- The level of difficulty should be challenging but achievable, and all the tasks should be measurable. If they are not, consider sending the Scouts out with digital cameras or camera phones so they can get evidence.

- You should include some 'maintenance tasks' to make the hunt harder. This could mean being in a certain place at a certain time, mini-deadlines put in before the main deadline, etc.

Notes

Though you do not need to supervise each group the whole time, you may like to have adults walking the local area (especially locations built into the task) so that some monitoring can go on and people can answer questions during the game if necessary.

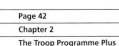

RECYCLING SCAVENGER HUNT

You must return to the Meeting Place at............................ **with as many of the following items or tasks completed. All tasks are worth five points unless otherwise stated. Good luck!**

1. A rap of over 50 words about recycling
2. Signatures of five people (not in your team) who recycle on a weekly basis
3. A recycling bag/box (NOT to be taken from a stranger's house)
4. The phone number of the local council
5. Three items found lying around that CANNOT be recycled
6. Ideas for how you can REUSE the three items in task five
7. A photograph with someone whose name is Green
8. The whole team up a tree
9. Some compost!
10. Recycled paper or toilet paper
11. An out of date telephone directory

You must also complete the following tasks and provide evidence for these:

1. Scavenge and recycle: (one point each)
a. A green bottle
b. A newspaper
c. A shoe
d. Three plastic bags
e. Clear glass

2. Your whole team must be at the town hall at 8pm to perform your rap. Lateness means failure! (10 points).

3. You must list your location, either by marking on the map or recording the grid reference on the back of this sheet, for every 15 minute interval of the task.

4. Find a man dressed from head to toe in green and get him to sign this sheet (12 points).

Remember to be back at the Meeting Place by ....

You will lose one point from your total for every minute you are late.

WEEK 7 - SPLASH!

As an island nation, water has played a large part in our history. Water activities learnt through Scouting can play a role in building the confidence of young people on the water. Many campsites offer raft building as a fun starter activity, but you can also do sailing, waterskiing, narrow boating and even offshore sailing as part of Scouting. This programme may work better as a weekend activity, but could feasibly happen as part of the normal meeting schedule.

You will need

- Boating equipment
- Safety equipment
- Relevant permits/permission

Programme Zones:	Outdoor and Adventure, Fit for Life
Methods:	Activities outdoors, Games
Links to badges:	A range of water activity badges (See below)
Preparation time:	Arrange activity with Water Activity Centre or local adults who hold permits for your chosen activity
Location:	Outdoor – at a water activity centre or on local waters.

Timetable

Time	Activity	Additional Information	Run by
18:00	Arrange to meet early at Meeting Place or at normal time at water activity location		
19:00	Safety briefing	Cover use of buoyancy aids or life jackets.	
19:15	Water activity	Usually booked in one hour or 90 minute sessions	
20:45	Return to Meeting Place or pick up from venue		

ACTIVITY DETAILS

- Local facilities will be the major factor in choosing which activity you will try. It is worth asking local Leaders what other Troops are doing on the water, as there may be opportunities that you haven't heard about.

- You will also need to ensure that the adults taking Scouts on the water have the necessary qualifications - Scout Adventurous Activity Permits or National Governing Body awards of external agencies. Use the Adventurous Activities Checklist on www.scouts.org.uk to do this. NB: Permits are not required for activities taking place on Class C waters, but you must inform your District Commissioner.

- Your Scouts will have opinions on what they want to do, so use a Troop Forum or discussion at the end of a meeting to get their ideas and run your ideas by them.

- If you have access to your own canoes or boats, combining the activity with a Night Away can provide unforgettable experiences. Remember that Hikes Away and Nights Away badges are available to those who complete a 'journey with a purpose' or an overnight stay with the Troop. If choosing this option, set aside some time to instruct Scouts in how to carry their belongings, stowing them safely and properly in the vessel chosen.

- Once the Scouts are on the water and have mastered the basics, devise a game or give everyone a course to navigate so that you are not just idly paddling or sailing around. Giving the activity some direction will make it more purposeful and engage the Scouts in using their new found skills.

Badges for water activities

Canoeist   Dinghy Sailor   Dragon Boating   Basic/Advanced/Nautical Skills   Power Coxswain   Pulling   Watersports

WEEK 8 - PIONEERING PROJECT 1

Pioneering is a traditional Scoutcraft activity that requires teamwork, strength, precision, discipline and good knowledge. There is great merit in building up your Group equipment to enable you to attempt more ambitious pioneering projects. This programme, to pioneer a swinging derrick, requires five blocks for making pulley systems, but apart from that the equipment should be easily on hand for you to use. Most Scout Activity Centres will have pioneering equipment able to cater for this programme, and possibly people with the know-how to help lead the session.

You will need

Ropes:

- 1 x 2-inch 60-foot to 100-foot
- 1 x 2-inch 50-foot
- 2 x 1-inch guide lines approx. 60 foot.
- 7 x 15-foot lashings
- 3 x 20-foot lashings

Spars:

- 2 x 12-foot to15-foot
- 2 x 3-foot to 5-foot

- 2 x pickets for anchoring guide lines
- 2 x double sheave blocks
- 3 x single sheave blocks
- Sacking for tree
- Plank for chair
- Sisal for mousing
- Step ladder
- Sledgehammer

Programme Zones:	Outdoor and Adventure, Creative Expression
Methods:	Activities with others, Activities outdoors
Links to badges:	Pioneer Activity Badge, Outdoor Challenge
Preparation time:	Sourcing and collecting equipment – 20 minutes
Location:	Outdoor – in area with suitable tree and/or stream

Timetable

Time	Activity		Additional Information	Run by
19:00	Opening Ceremony		Explain purpose of evening, and that Patrol Leaders will be elsewhere for the meeting.	
19:15	Patrol Leaders	Rest of Troop	Use plans to instruct Scouts in pioneering this versatile crane.	
	Troop Leadership Forum - To plan programme for next week	Build a swinging derrick		
20:30	Crane relay			
20:55	Closing ceremony			

ACTIVITY DETAILS

The easiest way to understand pioneering structures is to study them in action or to get hold of detailed drawings, so that you can count the parts needed and the number/type of lashings. The illustration of a derrick on a tree gives a good impression of how the crane works and is supported.

The parts needed for this project are listed above, but there are variations and extensions of the derrick you may wish to consider (see diagrams overleaf).

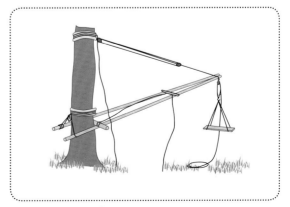

Swinging Derrick

- Ensure every Scout gets the chance to do a lashing or work on fixing a part of the project together. It may be worth having a 'lashing workshop' going on at one side with some extra spars, for those Scouts that don't know how to lash. Once they are confident they can join the project and get to work!

- Check every lashing. Remember that your derrick will ultimately be carrying Scouts over water.

- Give some instruction about the types of trees that are suitable to pioneer from. A general principle to stick to is to steer clear of dead trees (with the exception of oaks, which are very secure) and avoid crack willows (the Latin name *salix fragilis* will give you a clue why!) Alders are good riverside trees to choose, as well as other birches and beech trees.

- Make sure the guide lines are driven into the ground securely with the pickets. You should supervise this, and make sure Scouts using sledgehammers are properly trained.

Once you are happy with your crane, test it out over land, before putting it to use by a stream or river. You can then play a simple relay game using tokens and a stopwatch, which will test the Patrols' teamwork skills as they work against the clock to fulfil a simple task...

Glossary of terms

Derrick – A hoisting machine consisting usually of a vertical mast, a slanted boom, and associated tackle; may be operated mechanically or by hand.

Jib –
a. The arm of a mechanical crane
b. The boom of a derrick.

Boom – A long pole extending upward at an angle from the mast of a derrick to support or guide objects being lifted or suspended.

Lashing –

a. A method of binding or tying two poles together
b. The cord or rope used to tie the lashing

Picket – a pointed stake often driven into the ground to support a fence or other structure

Mousing – A binding or metal shackle around the point and shank of a hook to prevent it from slipping from an eye.

Sheave – A wheel or disk with a grooved rim, especially one used as a pulley.

Crane relay

- Split the Section into Patrols.

- The first Patrol operates the crane to lower one Patrol member down to the riverbank or above the river surface.

- The Scout on the Bosun's chair picks up a token (such as a coin or a coloured disc) and is raised back to return to the shore.

- They then place the token in a basket or suchlike, before returning to the Patrol, who have in this time switched positions and have another member prepared on the seat.

- The Patrol continue in this manner, capturing as many tokens in a five minute time period.

- After the time has elapsed, check the strength of the lashings and make necessary adjustments before the next Patrol begins.

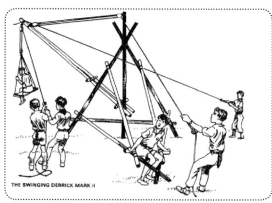

THE SWINGING DERRICK MARK II

You can extend this project by trying out John Sweet's 'Swinging Derrick Mark II' from his book *Scout Pioneering*. Then try your own modifications to make the crane even more useful. This is an ideal occupation for a week-long summer camp.

Badge links

Scouts showing a full involvement in this pioneering project will satisfy requirements 1b) and 2d) of the Pioneer Activity Badge.

WEEK 9 – GAMES NIGHT

As rewarding as it is to do programmes that lead to badges, it's sometimes good just to have fun and play games. To develop leadership skills in your Patrol Leaders or older Scouts, leave the planning and running of the programme up to them. They will relish the opportunity, and you will hopefully have a less tiring meeting!

You will need

- Balls
- Bats
- Cones/markers
- Rope
- Dice

NB: The Patrol Leaders could ask for anything to run their meeting, so in the planning phase show them the equipment readily available to the Troop so that they plan games with this in mind.

Programme Zone(s):	Fit for Life, Beliefs and Attitudes
Method(s):	Games, Team-building activities
Preparation time:	Planning with Patrol Leaders, setting up games (which can be done by Patrol Leaders)
Location:	Indoor/outdoor – normal Meeting Place

Timetable

Time	Activity	Additional Information	Run by
19:00	Opening Ceremony		
19:15	Hand over to Patrol Leaders	The Patrol Leaders could use any programme structure, but it is likely to keep the whole Troop together in competitive or cooperative games.	Patrol Leaders
20:45	Closing ceremony		

ACTIVITY DETAILS

If you are a new Leader, or running a new Troop, the prospect of handing over your meeting to young people to run may sound like a horrific idea! However, it is not long since the running of Scout meetings was generally considered the responsibility of the Patrol Leaders. Times and age ranges have changed since then, but it is still an important principle to maintain that young people have and should have an ownership over the programme they participate in.

For the meeting to be a success, you will need to work alongside the Patrol Leaders to plan what they are going to do. Use the 'Generating Ideas' techniques from pages 34-36 of *The Troop Programme*, write down all the ideas they come up with, then encourage them to choose the best ones, and begin to fit them into a meeting programme.

The phrase 'no idea is a bad idea' is a good one to use. However, it may be that some ideas are impractical and you will not be able to include them. The Patrol Leaders should enjoy the planning phase as much as the meeting itself, and you should try and bring out their decision making and leadership skills as they begin to add detail to the programme ideas.

The free-to-download resource *Scouts ... Taking the Lead* may come in useful when working with older Scouts. You can find this at www.scouts.org.uk/takingthelead

Once the meeting has been planned, get the Patrol Leaders to make a note of what equipment is needed and check that you have this in your equipment stores or it can be procured in time for the meeting.

We suggest the planning phase takes place during meeting eight, while the rest of the Troop are working on the pioneering project.

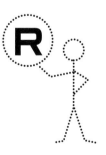

Badge links

Promise Challenge – I – Successfully run a learning experience for other Scouts.

IDEAS FOR GAMES

ZIP! ZAP! BOING!

This is an energy game to start things off.

- The Troop stand in a circle facing in.

- The object is to move energy around the circle in one of the following three ways:

    - Zip! - With the flow of the energy, pass to the person next to you, point fingers in direction of energy, shout 'ZIP!'

    - Zap! – Pass the energy across the circle, clasping hands and pointing fingers like a gun, lunging forward, making eye contact with recipient and shouting 'ZAP!'

    - Boing! – Repelling energy that is zipped towards you, raising arms, facing person who has zipped you, jumping and shouting 'BOING!' in the style of a spring.

Rules

- You cannot 'boing' a 'zap.'

- You cannot 'boing' a 'boing.'

- Hesitation, saying the wrong word, unenthusiastic actions and other tomfoolery can mean that you are out.

- Once everyone has got to grips with the manoeuvres, start whittling down the group whenever a mistake is made

- The people who are out can sit inside the circle formed by the players so that they are involved in the game as it reaches its conclusion.

- This game lends itself to adaptation. Change the words mid-game, introduce new gestures/words, whatever the Scouts come up with and can handle!

VOLLEY THE SPLOD

This is best played outdoors, and is essentially volleyball with big teams and water balloons.

- Fill 100 or so balloons with water and store them temporarily in two large plastic buckets/containers.

- Put the containers at opposite ends of a volleyball court you have marked out.

- The teams take to the court (they should ideally fill as much of the court space as possible).

- One team serves by throwing the first balloon over the net (height is important).

- A member of the other team catches the balloon (or not). If caught successfully they have to throw it to a member of their own team who in turn throws it to another member of the team, who throws it over the net. If anyone fails to catch it, they normally get soaked!

- The game continues in this manner until all the balloons are burst. Players should take turns serving.

- Score the game like conventional volleyball. However the Scouts are likely to be less concerned with who got the most points and more concerned about who is still dry. Normally a water fight ensues, so be on your guard if you don't want this to happen!

THE HUNT FOR THE TRUTH

This is an orienteering treasure hunt that spells out a message of truth…

- The Patrol Leaders hide luggage tags with letters on at several places in the vicinity of the local community.

- To help the Scouts find each tag, the Patrol Leaders think up a clue to lead them there (cryptic or general knowledge).

- On each tag, a letter is written. The letters should spell out a message, such as 'PLs ARE THE GREATEST.'

- The clues get written out on a sheet and copied for each Patrol.

- The Patrols (minus the Patrol Leaders) are given a clue sheet and map and have a certain time limit to hunt for wisdom.

- To add some spice, the Patrol Leaders patrol the game area with water pistols!

- The first Patrol to decipher the message is the winner

- This game has the potential to improve local knowledge, as well as fitness and team working skills.

- You may like to 'supervise' the game and it helps to set ground rules about behaviour in the community and non-contact!

Note

There are more games ideas on page 80.

WEEK 10 – JAMBOREE-ON-THE-TRAIL

Outdoor international activities can be challenging to organise. Jamboree-on-the-Trail (JOTT) is a global hiking activity that started as an idea in Canada in 1997. The basic premise is that on one particular day, Scouts plan a route to hike, knowing that this is happening elsewhere in the world. JOTT can also bring Scouts from other countries together, through message boards on the Internet in the planning stages. Register your Troop for JOTT and see what fun and friendship unfolds…

You will need

- Registration form from www.jott.org
- Personal hiking equipment (bags, clothing, etc.)
- Maps
- Compasses
- Wet weather gear

Programme Zones:	Global; Outdoor and Adventure; Fit for Life
Methods:	Activities outdoors; Activities with others; Visits and visitors
Links to badges:	International Friendship Partnership Award; Hikes Away; Global Challenge (Area 1)
Preparation time:	Registration online and networking with other Scout Leaders to plan route. Plan travel and budget. Sending out letters to Troop and collecting money. Booking campsites (if required)
Location:	Somewhere in the world!

ACTIVITY DETAILS

- Meet with other Leaders from your Group at the earliest opportunity to decide how wide your participation in JOTT will be. This could be a whole Group event, just for a few Sections or a linking event for Scouts and Explorer Scouts, for example.

- Fill out the registration form (you can download this from www.jott.org) and send it to the UK Coordinator (details on website).

- Start planning your trail. This could be somewhere local to you, but on the official JOTT date, or you could contact a Troop in another country and start planning how you will hike with them, or make contact with them during your JOTT activity.

Note: For details on how to make international links with Scouts, go www.scouts.org.uk/international well in advance of your JOTT event.

- Get all the necessary permits and forms for your hike sorted, using the Home Contact system where necessary.

- Inform Scouts about the hike, and prepare them for what they will need to carry with them. They may benefit from practicing walking with a rucksack if they have not done this much before.

- After the event, post your report on the website to tell others what your Troop did for Jamboree-on-the-Trail.

Notes

- Don't make your trail too ambitious for your Scouts. You may like to have two levels, so that the more experienced Scouts carry out a more difficult route or hike for longer. You should aim to be walking for at least four hours, so that you can count your JOTT activity towards a Hike Away.

- The Worldwide JOTT date is always a Saturday, so this leaves you with the perfect opportunity to build your programme around a Night Away. You could try out a new Scout campsite, or get to know unfamiliar terrain near to a favourite camping spot.

- Try to give the Scouts as much input into the route planning as you can. Those with good navigation skills and hiking experience could be given the responsibility to plan the whole route for everyone, or you could break into smaller hiking groups as long as everyone meets back at the campsite for dinner.

JOTT celebrated its 10th anniversay in 2007

Badge links

Hikes Away

International Friendship Award

Nights Away

Global Challenge

PROGRAMME PLAN TERM 3

THIS TERM COVERS ALL THE ZONES AND WORKS TOWARDS FIVE OF THE CHALLENGES, COMPLETING THE COMMUNITY CHALLENGE AND THE FITNESS CHALLENGE. SCOUTING SKILLS COVERED INCLUDE SHELTER BUILDING, EMERGENCY AID, PIONEERING AND HIKING.

You will spend at least one Night Away and complete one Hike Away. Three of the programmes involve visits or visitors and you will need to arrange extra adult help on three occasions. This term you will link with the Explorer Scout Section and invite parents to help with the Bake-a-thon. You might meet away from the Meeting Place in weeks seven and 10. An unusual item you may need to purchase in advance is a parachute.

Week	Programme	Zone	Methods
1	A night in Ancient Rome	CE / F	T / TBA
2	Scouting Skills	OA / G / BA	AwO / TNS
3	Spies	CE / F / OA	T / TBA
4	Campfire with Cubs	OA / CE	AO / DC
5	Unihoc tournament	F	TBA
5b	Up and down camp	OA	AO / PWR
6	Photo treasure hunt	C	TBA
7	Museum Visit - Duxford	C / OA	VV
8	Wide game	OA / F	AO / G
9	Geocaching	OA / C	AO / TNS
10	Unit takeover	C / BA	AwO / VV

Badge links

Term 3 – Summary
Ancient Rome
Scouting skills
Spies
Campfire with Cubs
Unihoc tournament
Up and down camp
Photo treasure hunt
Museum visit
Wide game
Geocaching
Unit takeover

SCOUTS

PROGRAMME METHODS / PROGRAMME ZONES

Programme Zones	Activities Outdoors	Games	Design & creativity	Visits & visitors	Service	Technology & new skills	Team building activities	Activities with others	Themes	Prayer worship & reflection
Outdoor & Adventure	✓	✓	✓	✓		✓			✓	✓
Global										
Community	✓	✓	✓	✓				✓		✓
Fit for Life	✓	✓	✓				✓			
Creative Expression		✓	✓	✓			✓	✓	✓	✓
Beliefs & Attitudes				✓						

The Bottom Line

Activity	Fun	Teamwork	Leadership	Relationships	Commitment	Personal development
○○○	○○○	○○○	○○○	○○○	○○○	○○○

1 tick = Poor
2 ticks = Good
3 ticks = Excellent

CONTACTS FOR THIS TERM'S PROGRAMME

ADC Scouts
Scouting Skills (climbing and caving)

Explorer Scout Leader (Young Leaders)
To get enough Young Leaders for week three and eight

District Commissioner
Activity approval

Cub Scout Leader
To organise week four

Imperial War Museum Duxford
Talk to education department to discuss trip

Air Activities Adviser or other Aviation Specialist
To run preparatory meeting

Other Leaders in the Group
To take part in Wide Game in week eight

Explorer Scout Leader
To organise week ten

CHECKLIST FOR TERM'S PROGRAMME:

1. Book campsite activities for term. ○
2. Book external providers. ○
3. Arrange date for Cub visit (campfire). ○
4. Arrange date for Explorer Unit takeover. ○
5. Write parent letter detailing weekend commitments (Up and down camp, Museum visit) ○
6. Re-stock First Aid kit. ○
7. Arrange extra adult help/Young Leaders for programmes two, three and eight. ○
8. Order badges from Badge Secretary. ○
9. Prepare/purchase materials for Spies programme and Wide game. ○

WEEK 1 - A NIGHT IN ANCIENT ROME

Following themes can be a crafty way of making activities that don't usually interest your Scouts more appealing. Here, a traditional meeting programme is followed, incorporating craft, public speaking, lashings and finally a chariot race in 'authentic' Roman headgear!

You will need

- Lashing lengths
- Pioneering spars
- Book of Roman myths
- Old bicycle/wheelchair wheels
- Sacking
- Safety helmets
- Gloves
- Pipe cleaners
- Crepe paper cut into 50cm lengths

Programme Zones:	Creative Expression; Fit for Life
Methods:	Themes; Team building activities
Links to badges:	Pioneer Activity Badge
Preparation time:	Prepare bases (10 minutes)
Location:	Indoor – normal Meeting Place

Timetable

Time	Activity				Additional information	Run by
19:00	Opening Ceremony					
19:10	Game – Romulus and Remus					
19:30	Bases					
	Bulldogs	Tigers	Woodpeckers	Eagles		
19:35	Rhetoric	Codes	Chariots	Laurel wreath		
19:50	Laurel wreath	Rhetoric	Codes	Chariots		
20:05	Chariots	Laurel wreath	Rhetoric	Codes		
20:20	Codes	Chariots	Laurel wreath	Rhetoric		
20:35	Inter-Patrol Chariot Race					
21:00	Closing ceremony and flag down					

ACTIVITY DETAILS

Romulus and Remus

- Play a traditional 'tag' game in the context of your Roman theme. The game starts with two Scouts who are 'it' and they are called Romulus and Remus, the twins who founded the city of Rome.

- Romulus and Remus have to catch as many other 'subjects' as they can. When they tag someone, they become a Roman. Everyone else is a free citizen.

- When a Roman is caught, they have to build the Empire by tagging other citizens and declaring them Romans.

- Romans join hands and chase others in groups of increasing size.

- Romulus and Remus can remain solo capturers for the duration of the game.

- The game ends when the Roman Empire has grown to include everyone. The last person caught can be declared the winner, or be thrown to the lions for outrageous resistance!

Rhetoric

Although a Greek invention, the art of speaking in public and constructing an argument or opinion was thought of very highly in Roman society.

- For this base, each member of the Patrol must speak for two minutes on a subject you give them. This could be related to Scouting, current affairs, or be completely random.

- Award points for how interesting their speech is, how well they manage to keep talking, avoiding repetition and keeping to the subject.

- Insist on polite applause at the end of each oration.

Codes

- Using an online translator or pocket dictionary, translate some Scouting words or phrases into pidgin Latin. The translations don't have to be 100% accurate as you are not trying to teach Latin, just to play a variation on a code-breaking game.

- Using these words and codes that are familiar to your Troop, write down the encoded words on separate pieces of paper and scramble these at one end of the room.

- The Patrol congregates at the other end of the room and one by one runs up to grab a code. They return to the Patrol who work at cracking it. They then make a guess at what the Latin word might mean.

- Have a list with the answers to refresh your memory. You may want to display the translations elsewhere in the Meeting Place for them to run to if they need to get the correct word before continuing.

- Continue to the next word and make a note of how many words are found in the time limit.

Here are some words/phrases you could use:

Castra aestiva	= summer camp
Sum paratus	= be prepared
Tentorium	= tent
Flamma	= fire
Vexillum	= flag
Fidelis	= loyal
Confido	= trust
Fortitudo	= courage

Make a laurel wreath

To add to the authenticity of the chariot race finale, use one of the bases to make laurel wreaths out of crêpe paper and pipe cleaners.

Instructions

- Cut a section of crepe paper that is about 50 cm long.

- Fold it lengthwise (so that it is still 50cm long, but now only about an 2.5 cm wide) and crease the folded side.

- Cut half-ovals or half-circles on the folded side. Leave a small amount (3mm) at one side of the shape, so that the paper remains intact, all along the length of the streamer.

- Wrap the streamer tightly around the pipe cleaner, leaving the half-shapes free and dangling. Fasten the paper to the pipe cleaner by folding the wire or taping it.

- Carefully unfold the dangling shapes, resulting in symmetrical leaves.

- Shape the pipe cleaner into a headband or crown. Secure it to the head with hair clips or simply by weaving the ends through the hair.

Chariots/Chariot Race

- In the base, Patrols have to design and build the most effective chariot they can to carry their lightest member and race around the Meeting Place

- The design criteria should be left open to different designs, but contain the following points:

  - Must be carried by Patrol members

  - The smallest Scout must be off the floor

  - Use at least two square lashings and be a free-standing structure.

- You could include wheels in your design, but you could design them so that the two main poles are left to drag along the floor (you may need to organise the course outside!).

- It may be safer to race two Patrols against each other and have a final. If however, you prefer 'controlled mayhem,' line all the Patrols up on the start line, Ben Hur style, and let the games begin!

See this and other craft ideas on
www.scouts.org.uk/pol

Tips

- Be careful to fold the crepe paper evenly, so that you don't accidentally cut past the edge and separate the paper.

- The tighter you wrap, the more realistic the laurel crown looks. If you hold the already-wrapped end of the pipe cleaner and let the streamer hang down, a tight wrap can be achieved by simply twisting the pipe cleaner. It's much more manageable than trying to flop the paper around the fuzzy wire.

- Half-ovals make laurel or olive leaves, half-circles make eucalyptus leaves - be creative with sizes and shapes to create different leaf types.

WEEK 2 - SCOUTING SKILLS

This matrix meeting will allow Scouts to pick up or refresh different Scoutcraft and camping skills in short 10-15 minute sessions. You will need knowledgeable adults to lead each of the suggested bases, who could be sourced if necessary from other Sections in your Group or others in your District. Contact your ADC Scouts to see how best to plug any gaps you may have. The codes activity is important as it will form a large part of the spy game in week three.

You will need

- Gas lamps/canisters
- Climbing rope
- Rope for tying knots
- Caving ropes
- Outdoor area with suitable tree for caving practice
- Pens
- Paper
- Football (indoor)

Programme Zone:	Outdoor and Adventure
Methods:	Technology and new skills; Activities with others
Links to badges:	Outdoor Challenge; Preparation for camp
Preparation time:	15 minutes before meeting to set up skills bases
Location:	Indoor/outdoor-based at normal Meeting Place

Timetable

Time	Activity				Additional Information	Run by
19:00	Opening Ceremony – reflection on skills					
19:15	Skills bases – explanation					
	Bulldogs	Eagles	Tigers	Woodpeckers		
19:20	Climbing	Caving	Codes	Lamps		
19:35	Caving	Codes	Lamps	Climbing		
19:50	Codes	Lamps	Climbing	Caving		
20:05	Lamps	Climbing	Caving	Codes		
20:20	Clear bases away					
20:30	Game – Crab multi-football					

ACTIVITY DETAILS

Opening Ceremony – reflection:

Ask Scouts to close their eyes and reflect as you read the following meditation:

Doing your best

Doing… It's impossible to do your best without doing things. Scouting gives us the chance to 'do'. Think of all the things you are able to do because you are a Scout. What other things would you like to do? Silently, ask God for new opportunities, and ask God to protect us in all that we do at Scouts. Thank you God for all that we are 'doing' at this meeting…

Your… God knows you. He knows your likes and dislikes. He knows your strengths and weaknesses. He knows your hopes and your fears. God knows you and cares about you. God made you as you are. Reflect on that, and ask God to help you achieve your potential through your time as a Scout.

Best … Everyone wants to be the best. They want to support the best football team, get the best results in an exam, be the best dressed, have the best haircut, drive the best car. At Scouts we ask you to do *your* best, not *the* best. God wants what is best for you, which isn't the same thing for everyone. Reflect on this… have you done your best recently? What things could you do better? Ask God to help you by giving you what's best for you today.

Open your eyes and think about what we've just reflected on, make the Scout Sign and say with me the Scout Promise:

On my honour,
I promise that I will do my best
To do my duty to God and to the Queen,
To help other people
And to keep the Scout Law.

Climbing – In preparation for the Up & down camp at the end of week five, take Scouts through the knots and techniques needed for climbing. This should include tying figure-of-eight knots, a bowline (including the method to tie a bowline around your waist). The correct way to wear a climbing harness, and how karabiner clips work. If necessary, invite the climbing instructor who will be running climbing at the camp to lead this base.

Caving – In preparation for the Up & down camp, use this base to introduce some of the techniques used when caving. This should include the single rope technique and can be practiced above ground using the proper equipment and a tree. Again, make sure that the person leading this base is properly qualified to instruct Scouts in caving.

Codes – Run through different types of codes and how to decipher them. This is important for the spies meeting the following week (but don't tell the Scouts this). Two codes to cover are as follows.

1 - Substitution ciphers

This is when the letters being deciphered (the key) are substituted by other letters (the clear). This is as opposed to transposition ciphers where the letters are the same but jumbled up or have other 'dummy' letters added. One way of doing this is to move the alphabet forward or backward by differing amounts, effectively giving the encoder 25 ciphers to choose from. Moving the alphabet forward five spaces gives you the following:

2- Anagrammatic codes

A simple way to send a secret message is to jumble up each word or even to write the sentence (punctuation and all) backwards. Using the latter, the second Scout Law becomes 'LAYOL SI TUOCS A'. To complicate the code, you can add an X to the end of every word and then move the first letter of each word to the end. Using this, the first Scout Law becomes:

'**XA COUTXS SXI OXT EXB RUSTEDXT**'. Variations on this theme exist to make the codes more or less tricky.

Once you have worked out the type of code, you are well on your way to cracking it. Once you have done this, you simply follow the formula carefully to find the solution. Allow time for Scouts to practice cracking codes. To help, you could prepare some quiz sheets in advance.

Lamps

As each tent will be given a gas lamp to use at camp when preparing for lights out, use this base to make sure every Scout is able to light the lamp, change the canister, change the mantle and store safely. (There is a Scout Skills Card available on this subject). You don't have to change a mantle every time if the lamps in your supplies don't need changing, but this is a good time to repair any lamps that need it.

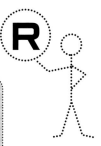

Order Scout Skills Cards from www. scouts.org.uk/shop

Clear	a	b	c	d	e	f	g	h	i	j	k	l	m	n	o	p	q	r	s	t	u	v	w	x	y	z
Key	F	G	H	I	J	K	L	M	N	O	P	Q	R	S	T	U	V	W	X	Y	Z	A	B	C	D	E

Using this code, the sentence '**I WILL DO MY BEST**' reads:

'**N BNQQ IT RD GJWX**'

And the enciphered sentence '**PJJV YMJ XHTZY QFB**' can be decoded (by moving backwards five spaces) to be:

KEEP THE SCOUT LAW

One way of deciphering substitution ciphers is by using a cipher wheel. This has an inner and an outer alphabet, and can be rotated the relevant number of spaces to find the encrypted message. To decipher, read from the inner (the key) to the outer wheel (the clear).

Crab Multi-Football

This is a great game to play in two teams to finish off the meeting. Instead of having one ball and causing a pile-up, play with multiple footballs. The referees can remove balls from play at any time and reintroduce them in different parts of the pitch to allow every player access to the game. The rules are the same as normal football, except players have to remain in crab position and move on hands and feet around the pitch.

Badge links

This programme serves as an introduction to climbing and caving, which could lead to a Climber or Caver Activity Badge.

WEEK 3 - SPIES

There are few themes as exciting to Scouts as espionage and the world of spies. Indeed the origins of the word 'Scouting' came from soldiers whose job it was to go ahead of their troops and gather intelligence about the terrain. Baden-Powell was very interested in spies, and introduced Kim's Game to Scouts, which was based on the spy character in Rudyard Kipling's novel, *Kim*. This theme night, which is a Patrol challenge from beginning to end, will provide a thrilling adventure while teaching some useful communication and problem solving skills.

You will need

- Pioneering poles (two 5m and four 1m per Patrol)
- Lashing lengths/sisal
- Rope
- One briefcase per Patrol (See below for contents)
- Pens/paper to make signs for jail, code clues, etc
- Mat/rug
- Keys
- Costumes (camouflage, dinner jacket, bow tie, etc.)
- Pre-prepared maps of local area (to give to Young Leaders and adults)
- Torch with wide beam
- Cloth/dark paper to black out Meeting Place for start of meeting

Programme Zones:	Outdoor and Adventure; Creative Expression; Fit for Life
Methods:	Themes; Games; Team-building activities
Links to badges:	None
Preparation time:	Need to plan route for 'stalking'; Produce sheets for codes and assemble props
Location:	Indoor/outdoor – around normal Meeting Place

Timetable

Time	Activity	Additional Information	Run by
19:00	Opening Ceremony		
19:15	Spy game begins	Needs one Leader to be jailor, one Leader to be captured agent, one Leader to be M, and other adults/Young Leaders to supervise activities	
20:55	Closing ceremony		

ACTIVITY DETAILS

- This Spy Game involves the whole Troop, who are split into Patrols or teams of five to six Scouts.

- The mission will be written inside a briefcase, which the Patrol will collect if they successfully complete the first game.

- To solve the mission the Patrol will need to use communication skills, lateral thinking, navigation, stealth, good local knowledge and Scouting skills.

Searchlight

- Before the meeting, set up the Meeting Place with obstacles and boxes to hide behind. You should plot out a logical route from the entrance door to the furthermost corner of the room and then either back to the entrance door or out another exit (depending on the layout of your building).

- In the middle of the Meeting Place, set up a table or two chairs, on which you will stand with a torch to rotate around the room. This is the 'searchlight.'

- Place a briefcase in the far corner.

- Hold the opening ceremony outside the Meeting Place, so that the Scouts do not see the room until they enter as part of the game. You may need adults on hand to collect bags/coats outside.

- Set the scene of the meeting, introducing the theme of spies and informing the Scouts that they are agents working for the government in the middle of an international crisis. They have to enter the facility and locate their briefcase which contains details of their mission. No more can be said at this time.

- One by one, the Patrols enter the room, trying to get to the briefcase and out of the room without being detected.

- Any agents caught in the searchlight are immediately arrested and sent to the jail (see Jail). The rest can continue and start the mission.

- Each Patrol will need a separate briefcase, which includes information for their mission, a mobile phone, some red herring material and fake identities (you can have fun making these!)

Mission

- You will need to prepare a mission briefcase (or equivalent) for each Patrol. This should include:

  - details of the mission typed with a typewriter or Courier font (see below)

  - a mobile phone (or borrow the Patrol Leader's phone just before the meeting, making a note of the number)

  - a photocopied (black and white) map of the local area. On this you will need to mark in red pen a start and end point (A and B) linked by a dotted line. This is the route you have planned for the Stalking mission.

  - fake identities, which will be tested if the Patrol are apprehended by 'police'

  - other, spy-related items, chosen at your discretion, but not essential for the mission.

Stalking

- For this activity, you will need to allocate one adult per Patrol to follow a prescribed route, dressed conspicuously, holding a film canister.

- Instruct these adults to begin their walk at a time you think the Patrol will be able to get to (by running) and to follow the course accurately.

- The adult needs to subtly drop-off the canister at a point about two thirds through their journey before stopping, looking around and continuing off.

- The map the Scouts receive should contain the route marked out in red pen, and they should have a space to mark the grid reference of the drop-off as evidence.

- Do not be tempted to use only one adult for all Patrols to stalk, and remember that the Patrols began their missions at staggered intervals.

- Inside the canister, fold a piece of paper with a diagram of a drawbridge on (see below).

```
Details of mission

A rogue agent is plotting mischief
in your locality. You must follow
him without being detected. Our
intelligence shows us he will leave a
film canister somewhere for an enemy
spy to pick up. This canister contains
classified information, and it is
imperative this does not fall into
enemy hands. Intercept the drop-off
using the map enclosed. When you have
the canister call M on . . . . . . . .
(phone number)

Good luck Agent 00-WOLF (Patrol name)
```

Round turn and two half hitches

Square lashings

5m poles

YOUR MISSION IF YOU CHOOSE TO ACCEPT IT...

Jail

- Any Scouts getting caught in the searchlight game are immediately sent to the jail – a room in the Meeting place you have set up accordingly.

- One Leader is appointed as the jailor. Their orders are to keep an eye on the captive agents, and not let them out. They are also told to fall suddenly asleep if they hear the word **'ANTELOPE'**.

- A key is placed under a mat in the cell. This is the key to the cell door.

- Once prisoners from any Patrol are in the cell, approach the jailor as another officer and have a conversation with them. During this, slip a crumpled note into the cell with the following written on it:

  MAX DXF MH MAX CTBE BL NGWXK MAX FTM. LTRBGZ 'TGMXEHIX' FTDXL MAX CTBEHK YTEE TLEXXI

- This is a cipher, which uses a code where the alphabet is moved seven places on, so A = H, N = U, E = L, etc. Deciphered, it reads:

  THE KEY TO THE JAIL IS UNDER THE MAT. SAYING 'ANTELOPE' MAKES THE JAILOR FALL ASLEEP

- On the wall of the cell, a piece of paper is displayed with a clue as to the rule needed to translate the cipher. This could be something like 'Move 7 on to freedom' or similar.

- Once a Scout successfully deciphers the code they send the jailor to sleep, find the key and leave the prison. After this, they can find their team by sending a text message to the Patrol Leader who has the secure phone and can text back their position. Two or more 'freed' Scouts can run out to find their Patrol together. If it is one lone Scout, they may have to wait for the Patrol to collect them after completing the mission.

Dial M for Message

- You will need to set up a mobile phone, so that when the Scouts call it you divert it to your answer-phone. You can know if a Scout Patrol is calling, by saving each Patrol Leader's number as the name of the Patrol in your address book.

- Change your answer-phone message so that it is coming from M, the mastermind of the operation, for the duration of the game. Remember to change it back straight away afterwards to avoid confused messages from your friends!

- The message should run as follows:
  'If you are hearing this message you have successfully intercepted the film canister. Well done. Agent 009 is in trouble. You must head to grid reference . . . . and await orders. For goodness sake keep this line open!'

- In the message, include the grid reference common to all the Patrols' maps that will lead them to the final destination of the game. This should be an open space such as park or common ground, with a tree or lamp-post in it. You will see why in the **Finale**.

- Make a note of when each Patrol calls, and find on your master map where they should be to intercept the canister. Estimate how long they will take to reach the finale grid reference, so that you can be there and send them a text message with their orders.

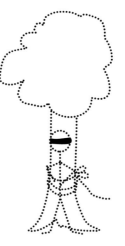

Finale

- In the finale of this espionage adventure, Patrols will arrive at the location you have directed them to (park or playground) to discover Agent 009 (a Leader dressed in tuxedo and blindfold!) captured and tied to a tree or post. All around them, a ravine is marked out by ropes, which is too wide for any Scout to jump across. Four to five metres should suffice. At different points on the outside of this area, equipment to make the drawbridge is in piles, one set for each Patrol.

- It would be good for you to be at the location, hidden from view, so that you can see the Patrols arriving

- When they arrive, send a text message including the following message:
!YLKCIUQ TCA. DESU SI TI EROFEB NOIRCURTSNOC RUOY EVORPPA TSUM Q. MARGAID EHT NI NWOHS SA EGDIRB EHT DLIUB DNA RETSINAC MLIF EHT NEPO, ENIVAR EHT SSORC OT

- This will fit in one standard SMS, and is simply the message backwards. It translates as:
TO CROSS THE RAVINE, OPEN THE FILM CANISTER AND CONSTRUCT THE BRIDGE AS SHOWN IN THE DIAGRAM. Q MUST APPROVE YOUR CONSTRUCTION BEFORE IT IS USED. ACT QUICKLY!

- For this exercise, Q should be dressed ridiculously in camouflage or suchlike and could be the adult who was tracked by the first Patrol of agents. They are called in to check that the Scouts have used all the correct parts and tied proper lashings before they use their bridge. Using benches on either or one side of the ravine will add to the sense of reality for the challenge.

- Essentially this part of the Spy Game is a race, but by sending the last Patrol to stalk a Leader closer to the finish, you will have created a level playing field and all the Patrols will have arrived on the scene by the time the game finishes.

- The agents cross the ravine, untie the knots and lead the captured agent to safety over their bridge and into a helicopter.

Notes

- Use Young Leaders/Explorer Scouts as police officers who can accost Scouts if they come across them in the game area. This will hold up the agents from making progress, and they will have to use their cover stories and persuasive skills to convince the police that they are innocent members of the public!

- You may need to build some code-breaking sessions into previous meetings if you don't think your Scouts will be able to crack the codes used throughout this game

- Though this is an outdoor meeting and best played in dry weather, giving advance notice and insisting on Scouts bringing waterproofs will mean you can go ahead whatever the weather.

- The Patrol Leaders should have the number of the mobile phone you are using to command the game. If not, programme it into the phone you place in each Patrol's briefcase and encourage them to use it if there is any problem during the game.

- This programme should easily last the whole meeting, but if your Scouts race through it and there is spare time, allow some opportunity to discuss their performance in the tasks, review their teamwork and communication and make suggestions for next time.

Badge links

Scouts playing an active part in this programme qualify for Area 4 of the Creative Challenge – Problem Solving.

WEEK 4 – CAMPFIRE WITH CUBS

Cooking on a wood fire at camp is a classic image of Scouting. However there can be great variety in the type of fire used, and it is an important element of Scoutcraft to reinforce in your programme. In the run-up to a camp, a practice session can greatly improve your Scouts' fire-lighting and cooking skills during the camp, saving your precious supplies of matches and paper. Make sure you meet somewhere with access to plenty of firewood, such as a local campsite, and why not invite the Cub Pack along so you can finish with a rousing campfire!

You will need

- Firewood
- Matches
- Fire grate
- Oil
- Frying pans/billies
- Eggs/things to cook
- Marshmallows
- Dough

Programme Zones:	Outdoor and Adventure; Community; Creative Expression
Methods:	Design and creativity, Activities outdoors, Activities with others
Links to badges:	Outdoor Challenge, Fire Safety Activity Badge
Preparation time:	Prior discussion with campsite staff, preparation of area for fire lighting and campfire.
Location:	Outdoor – local campsite or activity centre.

Timetable

Time	Activity	Additional Information	Run by
19:00	Opening Ceremony	Welcome Cubs and Leaders, put young people in small groups (could be mixed, or could have Scout Patrols and Cub Sixes)	
19:15	Fire Safety briefing	Everyone stays together to hear this as one group – explain three elements of fire triangle; what to do in an emergency; stop drop and roll technique; Troop Code of Conduct.	
19:25	Types of fire – marketplace format Altar fire Star fire Trench fire	If Cubs remain in Sixes they can do fire lighting first, and then perhaps altar fires. Encourage Scouts to keep moving around every twenty minutes or so. Have eggs, marshmallows, dough, etc.	
20:40	Campfire	Favourite songs – Cubs can teach Scouts and vice versa.	

ACTIVITY DETAILS

Fire safety

Refer to the Factsheet FS315076, *Scout Skills – Fire Lighting* and the resources for the Fire Safety Activity Badge. Both of these are available from the Scout Information Centre.

Types of fire

- The main aim of the meeting is to get an understanding of the advantages and disadvantages of different types of fire. Instead of timed bases, make things more relaxed by having all the fires running all the time. This 'marketplace' format is useful for activities that are difficult to allot time to.

- Scouts can learn about the fire(s) of their choice, but you should be encouraging people to circulate rather than spend the whole time at one fire. This way, the Cubs can also join in, but be directed towards the more basic constructions, as well as practice fire lighting.

Altar fire

In places where the turf may not be lifted or burned, an altar fire is often the only sensible solution for building an open fire. Raised from the ground on a wooden structure (as shown) or more usually on metal legs, the fire is made on top of a thick layer of earth or inside a metal drum. For this programme, build the altar fire shown in the diagram from scratch. You may wish to pioneer the base before the meeting, so that you get straight to the 'fire' part and can get the fire lit in the allotted time. Explain as you proceed that this fire is most like the conventional barbecue, and can cook a variety of ingredients.

Star fire

This is a small fire that maintains its size by moving three larger logs (the points of the 'star') towards the centre of the fire as they burn. The embers in the centre of the star are used for cooking. This fire is good for conserving fuel and backwoods cooking. It can be used with pots and pans by using a raised fire grate (on a stand). Once the fire is lit, experiment with different cooking styles and evaluate your results. You could easily have more than one fire on the go in your meeting.

Trench fire

This can be a very effective cooking fire, particularly on a hot day, as it keeps the heat of the flames below ground. Keep the windward end of the trench open, so that the prevailing wind blows into the fire, fanning the flames.

The Scouts should be aware that, despite its advantages, a change in the wind direction can mean that the fire loses its efficiency and a new trench must be dug. Not very good for a week long camp!

Campfire

It is no wonder that campfires remain so popular in Scouting. Everyone can sing their hearts out around the burning logs, and no-one cares how good or bad they sound – the emphasis is on having fun.

There will be no shortage of volunteers to be involved setting up the campfire, but if you are including young people in this, make sure they are absolutely aware of the dangers and that they know how to keep safe. Once the fire is going well, gather everyone around it on logs or benches, and start with songs that everyone knows, or are easy to learn.

Mixing traditional Scout campfire songs and chants with modern songs will work well. The Cubs may have a favourite that they can share with the Scouts, and vice versa. If you have time to prepare them, allow sketches to be performed.

Your focus should be on keeping energy and enthusiasm at fever pitch, while keeping the Cubs and Scouts at a safe distance from the fire, of course!

Badge links

Fire lighting and cooking forms part of the Outdoor and Outdoor Plus Challenge, based on the level of difficulty.

WEEK 5 – UNIHOC TOURNAMENT

Encouraging Scouts to be active can be a challenge. Many will be at an age where they need to be encouraged to exercise. A Unihoc tournament is an option that will appeal to Scouts; it is fast and furious and sufficiently different to school sports to seem exciting. As with the following details, it is a good idea to start the meeting with a quieter activity. They should be happy to sit down and check *Scout Record Books* and cards if they know that they will have the chance to dash about soon.

You will need

- Unihoc sticks (one per player, different colour for each team)
- Ball or puck
- Goal area x 2 (or jumpers/bags/ benches alternative)
- First Aid kit

Programme Zone:	Fit for Life
Methods:	Games, Team building activities
Links to badges:	None
Preparation time:	Setting up pitch = 5 minutes. Explaining rules and choosing teams = 10 minutes
Location:	Outdoors on playing field or park ground. Indoors at Scout Meeting Place, hall area

Timetable

Time	Activity	Additional Information	Run by
19:00	Scouts meet at Meeting Place Opening ceremony/flag break		
19:15	Inspection of *Scout Record Books* and Record Cards, updating of wallchart	To be done as a group. Leaders to verify information and Scout claims!	
19:30	Start of Unihoc tournament		
20:30	Finish Unihoc games, pack equipment away.	Favourite songs – Cubs can teach Scouts and vice versa.	
20.40	Announce the winning group	Record the winning team for future tournaments	
20:45	Return to Meeting Place/closing ceremony and short prayer		

ACTIVITY DETAILS

- Divide the Troop into teams. The number in each team will depend on where you are playing and how many people you have, but five to seven is about right. You can divide them up using a number of methods; having two captains; label each player with an odd or even number; match players by relative size/strength/age or Unihoc experience.

- Two teams compete each game, whilst the other players spectate (a Leader could be the referee).

- The length of each game can be determined by score (up to five), or by time (most points scored after 10 minutes of play).

- One Leader should keep track of the scores- a board can be used and kept for future tournaments (although this will mean keeping the same teams):

Team	Captain	1st game score	2nd game score	3rd game score	Tournament position
1	Bill				
2	Martha				
3	Ishmael				
4	John				

The order of play could be:

Team 1	Vs	Team 3
Team 2	Vs	Team 4
Team 3	Vs	Team 2
Team 1	Vs	Team 4
Team 3	Vs	Team 4
Team 2	Vs	Team 1

Notes

- Inspecting *Scout Record Books* might seem like an uneventful start to the evening. It is an activity that really should be done just once in a while. However, it is a necessary part of Troop life, and it might just make the Troop very eager to be energetic Unihoc players afterwards.

- Unihoc is a lively game; so remove fragile items from the playing area. Similarly, making a rule that the stick must be below waist height when the ball is struck will make the game safer. In Unihoc, players can tackle with either side of the stick.

- If you don't have access to equipment; using rolled up newspaper is a reasonable alternative. Arrange two teams to line up on opposing sides of the hall. Two players race each other, from opposite ends, to reach the ball first.

- An example set of rules for Unihoc can be found at http://eastyorks.boys-brigade.org.uk/competitions/unihocrules.htm - or agree on your own rules at a Troop Forum.

Badge links

- Physical Recreation
- Sports Enthusiast

WEEK 5B – UP AND DOWN CAMP

This sample programme for a weekend camp includes on-site activities that take Scouts above and below ground. Many campsites and activity centres offer climbing and caving, and high ropes courses are becoming increasingly popular. The timetable can be adapted, but provides you with a good framework for timings you can work with.

You will need

- Tents, dining shelters, Store tents, etc.
- Cooking equipment, utensils, food, etc.
- Flag pole and Union Flag
- Nights Away Permit

Resources: *Nights Away*, a resource published by The Scout Association, includes a chapter on equipment needed for camp as well as lots of technical advice, hints and tips for taking your Scouts away.
This is available from the Scout Information Centre (Tel: 0845 300 1818 or www.scouts.org.uk/shop)

Programme Zones:	Outdoor and Adventure, Fit for Life, Beliefs and Attitudes
Methods:	Activities outdoors, Team building activities, Prayer worship and reflection
Links to badges:	Outdoor Challenge, Adventure Challenge, Camper Activity Badge
Preparation time:	You will need to work with your leadership team to plan, organise and execute the camp
Location:	Campsite or Activity Centre

Day One

Time	Activity	Additional Information	Zone	Run by
19:00	Meet at Meeting Place and travel to site			
20:00	Arrive at site and pitch tents, unload equipment into stores		Outdoor and Adventure	
21:00	Cups of soup and hot dogs			
21:30	Play active game, e.g. Tails		Fit for Life	
22:30	Wash and lights out			

Day Two

Time	Activity	Additional Information	Zone	Run by
08:00	Breakfast			
09:00	Flag break and inspection			
09:30	On-site activities	Climbing wall Caving High Ropes	Outdoor and Adventure Fit for Life	
12:00	Lunch			
13:15	On-site activities	Climbing wall Caving High Ropes	Outdoor and Adventure Fit for Life	
16:00	Game: Four goal football		Fit for Life	
17:00	Special Meals – preparation		Creative Expression	
19:00	Serve and eat special meals			
20:30	Campfire		Creative Expression	
21:30	Hot chocolate			
22:30	Wash and lights out			

Day Three

Time	Activity	Additional Information	Zone	Run by
08:00	Breakfast			
09:00	Flag break and inspection			
09:30	Scouts' Own		Beliefs and Attitudes	
10:00	Team game		Fit for Life	
12:00	BBQ Lunch			
14:00	Strike Camp and Leave site			

ACTIVITY DETAILS

Caving – Those activity centres that offer caving on-site do so using caving tunnels purpose built for the centre, using instructors trained to use those tunnels. This is a relatively safe way to introduce caving to your Troop. However, there are risks and you will inevitably have to deal with young people who are scared to go underground into a dark, confined space. Encourage these Scouts to rise to the challenge and overcome their fears, and be sure to build on their achievements so that they grow in confidence. Check with the campsite what equipment/clothing is needed (you can expect to have to wear long sleeves and long trousers).

Climbing – Scouts love it, and there are many skills involved in mastering it, so it's a win-win. Making use of activity instructors on site takes away a lot of the headache in organising it, but many Troops have trained instructors with Permits who are able to instruct on your local wall or rock face. With the technique of belaying, Scouts can work together in pairs; and because what goes up must come down, you get the bonus activity of abseiling… for no extra charge!

High ropes – Not for the faint at heart, the trust games and walks played at height give Scouts the thrill and challenge of facing the unknown. This activity requires more courage than skill, but is perfect for building confidence and self-esteem with the great sense of achievement that comes from completing the course or jumping into the abyss. Make sure you book enough time for everyone to get a good go at this, and talk to the Scouts after their experience to maximise the Beliefs and Attitudes aspect of the activity.

Special meals – With no pressure on time at camp, running a Special Meals activity is an opportunity for Patrol Leaders to show some leadership skills and set up their own 'Hell's Kitchen' for the evening. The responsibility for planning the menu and ordering the ingredients can be left up to them, and they organise the rest of the Patrol to produce a meal the whole team can be proud of. Three courses, cultural cuisine, mandatory ingredients, add your own flavour to proceedings, but give the Scouts the freedom and time to come up with their dishes, and then enjoy them!

Scouts' Own – A Scouts' Own is traditionally a short service using reflections, readings, prayer and worship, in which all Scouts can participate whatever their personal faith. These services can be lead by a representative of a particular religion, by Leaders, or by young people themselves. Scouts working towards the Promise Challenge can plan a Scouts' Own to complete one requirement.

Make sure that the readings and songs chosen are inclusive of everyone, so that everyone can join in.

More information about Scouts' Owns can be found at www.scouts.org.uk

Badge links

Any camp is a good opportunity to start working towards the Outdoor Challenge and Camper Activity Badge. Because of the activities in this programme, Scouts would also gain the Adventure Challenge.

WEEK 6 - PHOTO TREASURE HUNT

The photo treasure hunt is an energetic, outdoor activity that allows Scouts to explore their local community. This programme idea is an excellent opportunity for Scouts to work together in small groups and actively search for things in the local area. The competition element combines well with being outdoors, and you should find that Scouts have enthusiasm for this activity.

You will need

- Cameras (one per Patrol or small group - preferably digital cameras)
- Route map of the area (one per Patrol or small group)
- Treasure hunt lists (one per Patrol or small group)

Programme Zones:	Community, Creative Expression
Method:	Team building activities
Links to badges:	Orienteer Activity Badge, Photographer Activity Badge
Preparation time:	30 minutes to 1 hour
Location:	Outdoors in the local community

Timetable

Time	Activity	Additional information	Run by
18:30	Scouts meet together at the Town Hall. Explain rules, distribute treasure lists and maps, divide into groups	Teams should be a mix of ages and experience. Patrol Leader to act as Leader of each team.	Leaders
18.45	Groups start the Treasure Hunt!	Make sure there is two to three minute gap between each group starting.	
20.15	End of activity, return to Town Hall. Read through the returned answer sheets – announce winner!		
20:30	Notices and meeting close		

ACTIVITY DETAILS

- Each team receives the table displayed. In their groups, they must find, and photograph the item described. The quality and accuracy of the photo can be judged afterwards, and points (between one to five) can be awarded.

- At each location, a clue will be hidden, usually a word or number. The team should record the clue at each location, and points can be awarded for each clue they find. To help everyone equally, give each team a route map of the area they will be hunting in.

- To make things more interesting, the clues can add up to a larger theme, something the groups can guess when they finish the Treasure Hunt.

Notes

- An important aspect of this programme is to provide opportunities for Scouts to work together in teams. The older members of your Troop have an important role to play in this, so encourage them to support the younger members of their team.

- Adults must be stationed along the route to help and guide the Scouts. Ensure each adult has a particular Patrol to keep an eye on. Stragglers can be urged on, and precious photo clues can be protected from overenthusiastic Scouts, members of the public, and the elements.

- The Troop must be reminded to be on their best behaviour when in public. Each Scout should wear at least a scarf.

- The clues you leave must be as unobtrusive as possible; it is possible that they could be removed if too prominent. It is also important to remove them as soon as possible after the Treasure Hunt is finished. For this reason, making the area relatively small is a sensible idea.

- Be sure to check for good weather before setting out the clues.

- Make refreshments available at the Scout Meeting Place, for when the treasure hunters come to photograph the front door.

Photo treasure	Picture taken (Y/N)	Score (1-5)	Clue found	Total score
1. The building with the '1667' date sign				
2. The White Horse pub on Exhibition Road				
3. The ice cream parlour next to the bus stand				
4. The front gate of the King John school				
5. The enormous tree at the entrance to Dean More Park				
6. The bandstand on the promenade				
7. The furthest side of the Town Hall building				
8. Underneath the Montford Road Bridge				
9. The foyer of Marks & Spencer				
10. The front door of Scout Meeting Place				
11. The noticeboard at the Civil Service building				
12. Bus stop F on Markway Avenue				

Alternative for next time

Now that the Troop are familiar with the activity, a variation is a Map Hunt, in which you provide a map of the area. Give clues to each team to find a series of 'treasures' on their way around. The first team back to the finish with all their treasure, wins!

Badge links

- Use of the map can help develop the skills needed for the Orienteer badge, the badge requirements and the Treasure Hunt programme require similar skills.

- May inspire the Photographer Badge.

WEEK 7 – MUSEUM VISIT – IWM DUXFORD (HALF TERM)

This example programme for a visit to a museum can be adapted, with the same principles used wherever in the country you may be and whatever the format of the museum. The best advice is to make contact with the museum before your visit. They may be able to tailor your excursion to your needs so that your Scouts get the best out of the visit. There may be hidden treasures, or exhibits that will lead towards badges. You never know – so ask!

You will need

Each Scout needs a daysack containing:
- *The Aviation Skills Quiz Sheet* (see appendix)
- Notebook/pencil
- Clipboard
- Camera (optional)
- Spending money (to buy models)
- Personal belongings
- Packed lunch

Per Patrol:
- Coloured pencils/pens (red and yellow)
- Information sheets used in previous meeting (see activity details)

Programme Zones:	Community; Beliefs and Attitudes; Outdoor and Adventure
Method:	Visits and visitors
Links to badges:	Aeronautics, Air Researcher, Air Spotter, Basic Aviation Skills
Preparation time:	Contact museum beforehand, arrange travel and possibly visit the museum yourself before to plan what the Scouts will do during their trip, timings, etc.
Location:	Imperial War Museum, Duxford

Timetable

Time	Activity				Additional information	Run by
	Travel to museum – give information about day on coach					
	Bulldogs	Tigers	Woodpeckers	Eagles		
10:15	Airfield	Museum	AirSpace	Museum		
11:15	Museum	Airfield	Shop/café	AirSpace		
12:15	Lunch					
13:15	AirSpace	Shop/café	Airfield	Shop/café		
14:15	Shop/café	AirSpace	Museum	Airfield		

ACTIVITY DETAILS

- The Imperial War Museum at Duxford is a world-class collection of aviation and military vehicles, giving plenty of opportunity for Scouts to learn about aviation history and national heritage. The museum has developed a range of Scout-focused educational resources, all of which turn your visit into a rewarding experience for all involved. This programme gives you all the information needed to plan and carry out your visit.

- The first thing to do in planning your visit is to contact the Education Department at IWM Duxford to find the best date for your visit. Call 01223 499341 to speak to a member of the team and they will send you the booking form. You could arrange your visit for a weekend, or a weekday during a school holiday (e.g. half term) – whatever is most convenient.

- Go online to download the pre-visit resources. These cover requirements of the Basic Aviation Skills Activity Badge that you won't be able to cover on the day of your visit. The museum recommend spending two to three weeks doing some of the activities before you visit the museum, but we have suggested an aviation themed meeting covering everything in one go. This will be suitable for a Troop with special interest in aviation (e.g. Air Scouts) but you may wish to adapt for your own Troop. The resources can be downloaded from http://www.duxford.iwm.org.uk

- IWM Duxford is in Cambridgeshire near junction 10 of the M11 – find directions at http://www.duxford.iwm.org.uk

- Scouts (Under 15s) go free, and by booking through the Department of Learning one adult for every six Scouts also gains free admission.

- It is advised that Scouts bring a packed lunch, which can be eaten in the picnic area inside AirSpace (if booked).

Museum – *The Basic Aviation Skills Quiz* will direct Scouts around the museum and its collections. Highlights include a large collection of British and American aircraft, the chance to see a Spitfire, the inside of a Concorde and a workshop where you can make your own glider (only available on weekdays). Give each Patrol enough time to see the bits they need to for the quiz sheet.

Airfield – The best way to learn about airfields and their rules is to see one in the flesh. Duxford, as well as being an aviation museum, has its own airfield. In fact, it played a key role in the Second World War as an RAF fighter station. You will be free to tour the airfield, as far as the control tower, in order to complete the third section of the quiz. You may wish to have an extra adult supervising groups as they walk around.

AirSpace – This is a £25m project, covering 12,000 sq ft of space and where the more hands-on exhibits are housed. Give each Patrol at least an hour here. The large jet engines here are definitely worth a look. There's also a conservation area, where aviation experts are restoring aircraft to their former glory ready to be exhibited. Again, talk to the education team if you wish to visit this area.

Shop/café – This is essentially a free-time session, where Scouts can buy gifts in the shop, look at bits of the museum they want to go back to, fill out their quiz sheets and visit the café.

You will need to collect in the quiz sheets at the end of the visit to see who has met the badge requirements. Those with gaps may actually know the answers, but you will need to draw these out through follow-up discussions. Make a note of any issues you want to go over at a future meeting, and build time in your programme to do this.

There will doubtless be Scouts who express an interest in aviation and want to take it further. The Basic Aviation Skills Activity Badge is the first in a series of three, each of which get more difficult. Sit down with the Scouts to see who wants to attempt the next badge. There may be Air Activities Advisers or flying instructors in your County who will happy to help get Scouts in the air.

List of resources and when to use them

Before	Airfields	Diagram labels answers markings and signals
	Meteorology	
	Aircraft	Parts of the aircraft – questions Parts of the aircraft – answers Aero Engines
The Visit	Quiz	Question sheets (1 each) Answers (1 per group/adult)
	Gliders	Balsa glider sheets for Make and Glide workshop

Of course, there are many aviation museums nationwide that can offer similar visits, and possibly Scout discounts. Some of these will also adjoin airfields and may offer flying or gliding as an activity. This may be the first time a young person in your Troop has had the chance to fly, so be prepared for some anxiety (followed by the overwhelming sense of achievement! For a list of UK Gliding Clubs go to www.esgc.co.uk

For your preparatory meeting, try and involve at least one aviation enthusiast in running things – such as a County Air Activities Adviser, a local Air Scout Leader, or even a member of the nearest flying club, Air Training Corps, or RAF base. Another good organisation to contact is the Youth Training Strut of the Popular Flying Association, which makes flying accessible for young people. Visit www.pfa.org.uk for more information.

This meeting uses three 25 minute sessions to get across the theory, with a team quiz at the end. There are no Patrol activities; everyone stays together. You may prefer to use bases, but that would normally depend on how many knowledgeable adults you have in your Troop.

Preparatory Meeting - Timetable

Time	Activity	Additional Information	Run by
19:00	Opening Ceremony	Introduce visitor/theme	
19:15	Aircraft Parts of a plane How aircraft fly Engines	See Scout Skills Cards available from www.scouts.org.uk/shop	
19:40	Game - Airplane!		
19:50	Airfields Draw diagram Labels Signals and communication		
20:15	Game – 2 minute paper plane challenge		
20:25	Meteorology Wind Ice Clouds		
20:50	Closing Ceremony	Give out details of trip to Duxford (meeting time, what to bring, etc.)	

Session one – Aircraft

Your aviation specialist will use a model aircraft to point out the key parts of a plane to include: nose, fuselage, tail, main-plane, port and starboard as well as the control surfaces of an aircraft. You could also use the *Scout Skills Cards*, which have diagrams of labelled aircraft. The session goes on to include a lesson in aviation theory and information on engines, which is covered on the information sheet.

Game – Airplane!

This is basically Port/Starboard (see page 80) but adopts an aviation theme, for example:

Nose dive – fall to floor

Roll – forward roll

Parachute – hands in the air, sway from side to side

Altitude sickness – mime being sick

Turbo jet – run really fast

Port/Starboard/Nose/Tail – different ends of room

Scouts can come up with their own linked suggestions, which you can add to the game as you go!

Session two – Airfields

Your aviation specialist draws the diagram of the airfield on a board or overhead projector. Point out the features one by one, explaining their function. Allow questions, and note which parts are no longer used and what has replaced them. Use the resource sheets to test the Scouts' knowledge. Finish by introducing some of the signals and communication methods used on airfields.

Game – Two Minute Paper Plane Challenge

Give each Scout a piece of A4 paper. They have two minutes to make a paper plane of their own design. At the end of the time, line the Scouts up at one end of the Meeting Place in groups of 5-6. The first group launch their planes. Make a note of the furthest one and to whom it belongs. Continue until each of the groups has thrown. If desired, give the Scouts another two minutes to improve their design and throw again. What designs work best? Why?

Session 3 – Meteorology

Use the sheets to go through the weather features that apply to flying and what aviators need to be aware of. Ask the questions on the sheet and see what answers are given. Reinforce the correct answers and answer Scouts' questions. Tell them they will be tested on their knowledge during the trip to Duxford.

> **You will need**
> - You will need
> - Model aircraft
> - Resource sheets (see above)
> - A4 paper

> **Badge links**
>
> This meeting combined with the visit has the potential to complete all the requirements of the Basic Aviation Skills Activity Badge and can ignite an interest in aviation that will lead towards other Aviation Badges.

WEEK 8 – WIDE GAME

Themed, outdoor wide games provide Scouts with original opportunities to practice teamwork, physical pursuits, problem solving, tactics and skill - all within the framework of a structured game. Give this mythology-themed game a go and see your Scouts transported into a world of unicorns, barons and elves!

You will need

- Seven adults
- At least six+ Young Leaders/Explorer Scouts
- Several old/blank CDs
- CD marking pen
- Two tent pegs (spray-painted silver if possible)
- Map (see preparation)
- Wool/masking tape for lives
- Riddle sheets
- Small groundsheet/ tarpaulin (one per Patrol)
- Sisal/string
- Blue climbing rope or aluminium foil
- Folding chairs for adult helpers
- Equipment for making assault course

Programme Zones:	Outdoor and Adventure; Fit for Life
Methods:	Activities outdoors; Games; Team building activities; Themes
Links to badges:	Outdoor Challenge
Preparation time:	20 minutes to brief adults/helpers, 30 minutes to set out game area (with help) and hide treasure/clues
Location:	Outdoor, in wooded area that you can have almost private access to for the duration of the game. Busy areas of parks should be avoided, but campsites and woodland are very suitable to this activity

Preparation

Select the location carefully for your wide game. It should include a wooded area of at least two acres and open field. A local campsite, park or woodland should suffice. Trees are always important, to provide cover and simplify the 'roping out' of areas.

On the border/outskirts of the wooded area, at the four corners, mark out a small area as 'villages.' These will be the home bases of each team. This version of the game assumes four teams but you may have more/less.

Marking the area

At the centre of the 'enchanted forest', rope out another area as The Friendly Farriery. This should be larger than the villages, about twenty paces in diameter. You will also need a 'lake of life.' If there are no obvious water features in your wood, lay out a blue climbing rope, or improvise a lake with aluminium foil, and place a chair next to this.

Another area to mark out is the baron's castle. This should be at the edge of the forest, and marked out with sisal. Outside the castle's limits, but within view of it, hide/drape four small groundsheets/tarpaulins. These will be the unicorn saddles. Attach a label to each, marked A4.

On the opposite side of the wooded area, in open land, plan and lay out an assault course. This is the Royal Showground. If you are playing this game at camp, this area should be in closest proximity to your site. Otherwise, make this area the meeting point for the game, where you will be throughout to answer questions. If travelling to play your game, this area will be closest to the car park so that whatever equipment you need for the assault course does not need to be carried far. Planks of wood, scramble nets, cones and tyres will help make obstacles, and you should raid your Group's equipment store for useful objects. Alternatively, you may be playing the game at an activity centre, which has a ready-made adventure course you can use.

Drawing your map

The most important task in preparing the game is to draw an accurate map of the imaginary kingdom in which the game is to be played. This must have a grid, and contain all the parts (see page 73) necessary to the plot of the game. On top of this, mark out natural features of the park/wood that can act as points of reference to the Scouts during the game.

FInally, you will need to hide/bury the unicorn horns (wooden tent pegs sprayed silver or gold) in close proximity to one of the added features on your map. Once the Scouts find the grid reference they need and arrive at the feature, they should be able to follow a trail to the legendary horn. Therefore, lay tracking signs or a blindfold sisal trail or clues that will lead them from the grid reference to the 'X marks the spot' – use your imagination and embrace the theme!

You are now almost ready to begin the game. But first you will need to brief the seven or so adults and extra Explorer Scouts of their roles, and then explain the object of the game to the Scouts. Study the next pages carefully so that you fully understand the game yourself. You may wish to adapt aspects of it, either to simplify or further complicate. For example, the game is won by one team finishing an obstacle course fastest. However you may wish to give credit for the least number of lives lost, most riddles solved, tactical prowess and such like.

All Scouts will need to start out with lives around the top of the right arm. These can be tied with wool, or you can use masking tape to reduce the risk of injury when they are being pulled off.

Scenario

The game is set during the reign of King Ben, the elderly ruler of the kingdom of Tuocs. An evil baron has captured the rightful heir to the throne. There are rumours that the baron has been seen at an apothecary ordering a deadly poison. With the young heir being the only child of King Ben, any harm done will throw the country into chaos and disorder. The only hope is to find a unicorn, the horn of which is said to be able to revive anyone who has been poisoned. This task is not easy, as the baron's Black Knights guard the castle, and the only known habitat of unicorns is the Enchanted Forest.

NB: This version of the game assumes four teams.

Aim of the game

The Troop is split into teams of five to six Scouts. These teams collect items to build a unicorn, which they must take to the royal showground and parade before the King. They must avoid being caught by the Black Knights, who serve the dastardly baron.

Time allowed

The game will take up the whole meeting, and could alternatively be played during a camp or residential experience. The game is played in three stages. Stage one should take 30 minutes, stage two should take 20 minutes, stage 3 will take longer, as it requires some map reading, tracking and an assault course.

Beginning the game

Each team is taken to their 'village' – a small roped off area on the border of the Enchanted Forest, which is a safe haven for that team. In each village is one adult (the Village Chief) whose job is to hand out new lives, keep parts of the unicorn safe, offer strategic advice and remind hapless Scouts what their task is. This adult should have a copy of the rules to jog their memory.

The Chief gives their team the starting instructions on the back of a map that you will have drawn out (see next page).

Stage one – The Friendly Farrier and the Enchanted Forest

When the Chief gives each team their instructions, they are to wait for the signal (whistle, bugle, etc) that starts the game. After hearing this, the Scouts enter the Enchanted Forest to look for horseshoes. These are old/blank CDs that have been deposited in the area prior to the game. There should be enough for four per team with some left over. The Scouts take horseshoes that they find to the Friendly Farrier, whose smithy is inside the wooded area and marked out with rope (a safe area). When a Scout presents the Farrier with a shoe, he/she asks what team they are in and then marks the CD with a 'brand' that corresponds with the code on his/her list.

At the same time, Young Leaders/Explorer Scouts posing as Black Knights are in the area, trying to catch Scouts. If the Scouts are not in possession of a horseshoe, their life is taken and they have to return to the village to get a new one. If they have a horseshoe, this is taken from them, but they retain their life. Confiscated horseshoes must be returned to the Friendly Farrier. Appoint an adult to be the Farrier's Assistant, whose job it is to return confiscated CDs back into the game area, so that they can be found by the Scouts. (If you make this a task of the Black Knights, they might hide them too well!)

Once a team has four shoes, each with different codes, they are ready to progress to stage two. Teams keep going at this stage until they have four shoes (the Black Knights should ease off after 30 minutes to allow them to progress).

Stage Two – The unicorn's saddle and the Lake of Life

Legend has it that unicorns cannot be tamed, but these ancient writers did not know about the unicorn's saddle, which was crafted by an alchemist and possesses special powers. When the teams return to the village with all four horseshoes, they will head to the Lake of Life. This is a safe area inside the boundaries of The Enchanted Forest, inhabited by an elf. The elf (another adult) tells the team about the saddle, which has to be taken from the ground of the baron's castle. This is a perilous mission, as Black Knights patrol the grounds, and if caught, the Scouts will be thrown in the dungeon.

Scouts go stealthily to the castle, marked on their map. The castle grounds is a large marked out area, in which four groundsheets are visible, hanging from trees or on the ground. At the centre of this area is a smaller roped area. This is the castle/dungeon, in which sits another adult – the Evil Blacksmith. If Scouts are caught by Black Knights, they are taken here, where they have to correctly answer a riddle to escape. (See page 74 for riddles).

Stage Three – The magical horn and the final test

With the four shoes and the saddle, the team are now one step away from making their unicorn. Each of the pieces captured so far has a marking on it that will lead to the horn. See the completion key on the next page for how this works. The Village Chief can help them put the code together. This stage is more challenging: firstly, whereas there are shoes and saddles enough for each team, there are only two horns, so the team that gets there first will prevent another team from succeeding.

Secondly, the hiding place will be harder to find. The team will need to follow a trail, or answer questions, or read tracking signs in order to get to the exact place the horn is hidden. Depending on what you choose to do here, you may need extra adult help, or can reuse the adults who were the Farrier and the Elf. Once the two horns have been found, the successful teams proceed to the Royal Showground and a signal is sounded to tell everyone that the game has come to its climax and everyone must meet at the showground. The finale is an assault course for the finalists, who attempt it in unicorn formation (see diagram overleaf) – the fastest wins the game and frees the heir to the throne, restoring order in the land!

RESOURCES

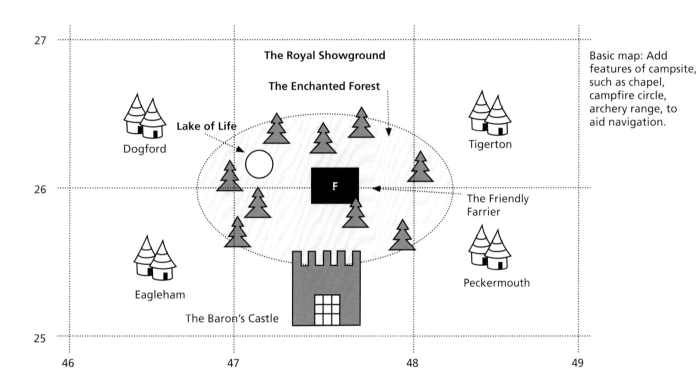

Basic map: Add features of campsite, such as chapel, campfire circle, archery range, to aid navigation.

Starting instructions

Go into The Enchanted Forest and find unicorn horseshoes. Take these to the Friendly Farrier who will verify them and brand them for you.

Beware the Black Knights, who will attempt to steal your shoes for their horses. Once you have four shoes, head to the Lake of Life, where an Elf will tell you of your next task.

Hints

Horseshoes are safe when they are in your village.

You are safe in the Friendly Farrier's Farriery.

You cannot take the life of a Black Knight.

Elf instructions

You must now find a unicorn saddle. These are hidden in the grounds of the evil baron's castle. Be careful! The castle is patrolled by Black Knights who serve the baron, and if you are caught you will be thrown in the dungeon.

Bring the saddle back to your village, so that you can begin your final task – the quest for the unicorn's horn.

Hints

If you are caught, you must answer a riddle correctly to escape the dungeon.

Unicorn saddles have the power of invisibility. If two or more of you are under the saddle, you cannot be captured.

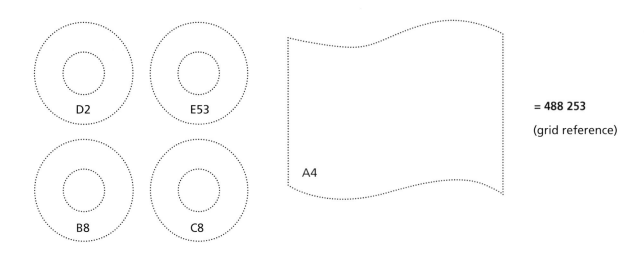

D2

E53

A4

= 488 253

(grid reference)

B8

C8

Diagram of Unicorn Formation

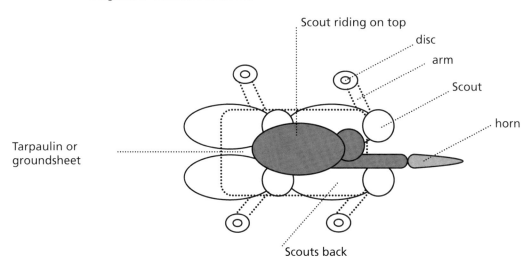

Scout riding on top

disc

arm

Scout

horn

Tarpaulin or
groundsheet

Scouts back

Riddles

When is a door not a door?
When it's ajar.

What's brown and sounds like a bell?
Dung

Why is six afraid of seven?
Because seven eight nine.

*Name three consecutive days without
saying the words Monday, Tuesday,
Wednesday, Thursday, Friday, Saturday
or Sunday.*
Yesterday, today, tomorrow.

*Which weighs more – a ton of bricks, or
a ton
of feathers?*
They both weigh a ton.

*What's been around for millions of
years, but is never more than a month
old?*
The moon

What am I?

My first is in WOMAN but never in MAN
My second in FRANCE, but not in JAPAN
My third is in LYNX and also in YAK

Add X for a beast you'd be a fool to
attack.

Answer: ORYX (an African mammal,
whose horns resemble that of the
unicorn)

*I am as light as a feather, but no man
can hold me for long. What am I?*
Your breath

Note: While riddles complement the fantasy
theme, they can be hard to solve. You may
prefer to use general knowledge questions.

Adult roles

Village Chiefs – hand out starting instructions; offer tactical advice; keep horseshoes/saddle safe; give out new lives; reinforce theme; give clues to how grid reference of horn can be found.

Elf – sits by lake of life and reads out the whereabouts of the unicorn saddle; they can be enigmatic when describing the whereabouts of the unicorn's horn (as Scouts are bound to ask).

The Friendly Farrier – This is a key role. They will need to mark the unicorn horseshoes with a code you give them, which gives the reference for where the horns are hidden. For example, if you are using the map on the previous page and there are four teams, and you know that the horns are hidden near the children's slide and the water fountain, the CDs should be marked as follows:

Tigers	B8	E53	D2	C8
Bulldogs	D5	C2	E3	B88
Woodpeckers	E2	C92	D4	B6
Eagles	B6	E2	C9	D24

The Farrier should cross off each alphanumeric as it is given out. As Black Knights can confiscate CDs, these may need to be reissued. In each case, the Black Knight should return the stolen CD to the farriery, so that you can keep track.

Black Knights – Explorer Scouts will enjoy their 'baddie' role in the game, but it is important that they play by the rules to prevent the game plummeting into chaos. For stage one, the aim is to catch as many Scouts as possible. This is made harder by the fact that the Scouts are coming from all directions. You should dissuade the Black Knights from all hanging around the area marked out for the Friendly Farrier, although some should surely patrol this area. In the second stage of the game, the Black Knights are the ones patrolling the castle grounds. They must make the decision how they distribute their forces as the game pans out. The important rule for the Black Knights is that they must return any CDs captured to the Friendly Farrier and then put them back in play fairly so that the Scouts can find them again. This is crucial, and should be made clear before the game starts.

The Evil Blacksmith – In the dungeon of the baron's castle, the Evil Blacksmith keeps guard. However, he/she is fascinated by riddles, and can grant the freedom of any prisoner who helps to solve one. This role requires a little artistic flair, and should aim to make being imprisoned more fun than it may sound. A list of riddles is below, but can be added to with any that you may know.

King Ben/Heir to the throne/The Baron – These characters are all mentioned in the game, but do not have a physical role. Therefore, you can either do without them, or if you have the adults to spare, they can be wandering the game area. It would be good to finish the game by seeing the rightful heir to the throne set free, and the baron punished. However this will depend on both the time, resources and energy that you have left!

Badge links

Outdoor Challenge

WEEK 9 - GEOCACHING

With the rise in popularity of both the Internet and GPS (or satellite navigation) a game was invented that combines the two. Best described as technological treasure hunting, Geocaching combines the traditional Scouting Skill of navigation with 21st Century technology, and is also a novel way of promoting Scouting in your local community. Interested? Read on...

Note

If this is your first time geocaching, you may find you need more time to do all the activities listed here than suggested.

You will need

- A GPS Receiver (hand held) such as Garmin eTrex
- Access to the Internet (can be before/after meeting)
- Hiking equipment (personal kit)
- First Aid Kit
- Ordnance Survey maps of area
- Compass
- Small items to leave in caches
- Old tupperware box/lid
- Small notepad
- Pencil

Programme Zones:	Outdoor and Adventure; Fit for Life
Methods:	Outdoor activities; Technology and new skills
Links to badges:	Navigator Activity Badge
Preparation time:	Research on Internet to find caches, practice visit, collating and printing resources for meeting.
Location:	Outdoor, dependent on proximity of nearest cache or caˆche you create.

Timetable

Time	Activity	Additional information	Run by
19:00	Opening Ceremony		
19:10	Introduction to GPS/Geocaching		
19:25	Start hike to find cache		
19:45	Arrive at cache location – hunt cache		
20:00	Place a cache		
20:25	Hike home		
20:45	Explain next steps		
20:50	Closing ceremony		

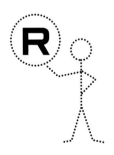

Preparation – If you have never used a GPS navigator before, or are unfamiliar with Geocaching, refer to the new Scouting Skills factsheet: *GPS Navigation* (FS 315089). This will teach you the basics.

A basic GPS receiver will cost £50-100. This may seem like a big expenditure, but there are many uses for GPS within Scouting, as an alternative to the compass. It is a good example of the 'technology and new skills' method and a way of getting from place to place that Scouts will no doubt find unusual and fun. In large Troops, start geocaching as a Patrol activity, on a rotational basis, until you are able to afford more receivers. As they grow in popularity, parents in your Group may have purchased their own and will be happy to lend them for the occasional Troop meeting.

Your preparation will involve researching caches in your local area. The only way to do this is to go online to a geocaching website to see what is around. The two most popular sites for 'cachers' are www.geocaching.com and www.geocache. co.uk. These list câches as well as providing useful advice and guidelines to get you started. Put in the postcode of your Meeting Place (or address on the search page) and the system will search for caches within a 100-mile radius, listing them in order of proximity. From the results returned, you will be able to decide where to start your meeting, enabling you to find at least one cache in the timeframe. Be sure to read the remarks of cachers, and how easy it was for them to find. The entry will also include hints of how to find it and other impartial advice from users.

It may be worth conducting your own trial visit to the cache before the meeting. This is mainly to check that you are able to use the receiver yourself and secondly to ensure that time is not wasted on the meeting hunting for a câche that is impossible to find.

Print off all the information you will need for the meeting, particularly the waypoint for each of the locations you are hoping to hike to.

ACTIVITY DETAILS

Using the factsheet, demonstrate to the Scouts how to programme the GPS receiver to track a waypoint (set of coordinates derived from the longitude and latitude system and not a map grid). Show the different functions of the GPS and what the different reading signify.

Find a cache

- Using the details printed from a geocaching website, plot the rough location of the cache on the map, and plan a walking route from the Meeting Place to the waypoint. Programme the waypoint into the GPS.

- Walk the route, referring to the GPS during the journey and asking the Scouts about its benefits and features.

- When you arrive at the location, the Scouts will enjoy hunting for the cache, normally a small container hidden in the hollow of a tree or under fallen wood.

- Once found, the Scouts will need to write in the logbook, exchange items if they wish and return it to its hiding place, as per the rules of the game.

- This should be done without drawing the attention of non-cachers, or 'mugglers!'

Placing a cache

- Firstly, you will need to agree on a suitable location. The criteria to keep in mind is that the place should be relatively easy to get to from a car park or station, so that dedicated cachers need not traverse miles of wilderness to get to the location. Not all geocaching is done by Scouts! You should also avoid privately owned land (unless you have permission).

- Once this is agreed upon, use the GPS to record your exact location.

- Make up the cache, using the pencil to note the first entry in the logbook. Attach the lid and perhaps mark on the outside of the container that this is part of the geocaching game and should be left if found by accident.

- Hide your cache.

- Someone will need to go online to log the cache on a geocaching website. The waypoint is the main detail needed, but there are other things to list. Make a note of all these before the meeting.

The next steps

- The process of logging each find and each cache placed should be explained to all the Scouts that have taken part. If the activity has been a success, you may have Scouts eager to take up geocaching as a hobby, or use it to work towards the Navigator Activity Badge. Geocaching may be a more appropriate activity for the weekends, as evening meetings will only lend themselves toward sophisticated treasure hunting during the summer months when it stays light longer. Perhaps you can come to an agreement of times when you will put geocaching on the programme. This could include camps.

- Talk about the environmental factors to consider when going geocaching. Why might it not be a good idea to place a cache? How can you find out who the landowner is? Tell the Scouts about the Geocaching Association of Great Britain (for England, Scotland and Wales) and how they can be responsible cachers.

Spreading the word

- As geocaching reaches a larger audience, why not use this activity to promote what you do? You may even gain some new recruits as a result!

- Photocopy the advertisement (below) and write details of your Group and how to join. Laminate this and you've got yourself a cache-sized promotional tool. Scouts may also like to use group nametapes or woggles as items to leave in the caches that they find.

⌐ **SCOUTS** ⌐

Scouting offers challenge and adventure to 400,000 young people and 100,000 adults across the UK. We believe in helping our Members fulfil their potential learning by doing and thinking for themselves. We give people of every background the chance to stretch themselves, learn new skills and make life long friends.

The Scout Section (for girls and boys aged 10½ - 14) helps young people work together in teams and try their hand at a range of exciting activities, such as geocaching!

Why not join the adventure and find out what Scouting has to offer you?

www.scouts.org.uk/join

Badge links

There is a GPS Navigation alternative to the Navigator Activity Badge.

WEEK 10 - UNIT TAKEOVER

It is likely that members of your Troop will be nearing Explorer Scout age. Many Scouts will be eager to see what the next Section has to offer. Asking an Explorer Scout Unit to run your Troop night is an excellent opportunity to introduce the members and activities of the Unit. The difference in age between the oldest Explorer Scout and the youngest Scout can be considerable and the meeting programme must reflect this difference. A good example includes team games, with activities that includes all members. The aim should be to provide a entertaining evening that introduces typical Explorer activities in an environment that is enjoyable for all.

You will need

- Straw Tower:
- Supply of drinking straws (50 per team)
- Sellotape
- Scissors
- Drawing pins (or paper clips)

Photo Show

- Projector and stand

All-in Dodgeball

- Sponge ball 2

Programme Zones:	Beliefs and Attitudes; Fit for Life
Methods:	Activities with others, Visits and visitors
Links to badges:	None
Preparation time:	30 minutes
Location:	Meeting Place - Indoors then outdoors

Timetable

Time	Activity	Additional Information	Run by
19:00	Opening Ceremony	Troop Leader welcomes Explorer Scouts to the meeting	Leader
19:15	Team activities - Divide Scouts and Explorers into Patrols (1-2 Explorer per group); introduce games	Led by Explorer Scouts	
19:20-19:45	Straw tower building		
19:50-20:10	Explorer Scout expedition show	Explorers show photos of their summer expedition	Explorer Scouts
20:10-20:45	All-in Dodge Ball	Leaders must supervise	
20:45	Activities finish	Use this time to let the Scouts and Explorers mingle; as well as relax after the activities	
21:00	Quick fall-in/notices/flag down Explorer Scout Leader addresses Troop	• Thank you to Explorer Scouts from Troop Leader • Give details of next joint meeting	

ACTIVITY DETAILS

Straw Tower Building

Using only straws, pins (or paper clips) and Sellotape, the teams must build the tallest possible tower. Distribute the materials and inform the teams that a prize will be awarded for the tallest tower built. Setting a time limit of 15 minutes (and a maximum of 50 straws) will really help the teams concentrate on this task.

Note

Having a mixture of older and younger members in the groups is essential. This helpful hint for teams can speed things up:

Demonstrate:

Three straws as a triangle

Four straws as a rectangle

Five straws as a rectangle

Explorer Expedition Photo Show

Explorer Scouts show the Troop photos of their summer expedition to Slovakia. This is an excellent opportunity to explain more about the exciting activities and expeditions that Explorer Scouts undertake.

All-in Dodgeball

One or two people (probably Scouts to begin with) become the 'taggers'. They must use the ball to 'tag' the other players below the knees. Once a player is tagged, they must leave the area and sit to one side. Eventually, only one player will remain: they win!

An interesting variation to consider is when one player is tagged; they switch places and become the tagger. You will need to impose a time limit on this game to ensure an ending. It is important that the balls used are soft and hard throwing is discouraged.

Notes

- Although adults must be present, the Explorer Scouts should lead the meeting. This is an opportunity to get to know the members of the older Section, and experience typical Explorer Scout meeting activities.
- The groups need to have a range of ages; the idea is for the older Explorer Scouts to guide the younger members. These activities are designed to get everyone talking and enjoy the meeting. Although the competitive element will always help motivate young people, it should not be too important.

Badge links

The straw tower building could contribute towards the Craft Activity Badge, particularly if it leads the Scout to completing similar craft activities.

GAMES

1. Untangle

- The whole Troop gathers in a tight huddle/circle.

- Everyone has to grab the hand of two other people in the huddle, so that everyone is holding hands.

- Shout 'UNTANGLE!'

- Still holding hands, the Scouts have to untangle so that they are standing in a circle.

2. Timebomb

- Mark out playing area (this game cannot be played in open space without boundaries).

- Throw the 'timebomb' (a beanbag or ball) to one of the players and begin counting down from ten to zero.

- The Scout with the timebomb has to catch someone else and pass the bomb to them. The others try not to get caught.

- Whoever has the timebomb when the count reaches zero is 'out.'

Rules

- When tagged, players have to accept the timebomb immediately and can be given out for not doing so.

3. Port and Starboard

- This is a classic game to get Scouts running around the Meeting Place, using a nautical theme. The theme and commands can be changed around with limitless possibilities.

- Scouts have to react to the following commands:

Command	Instruction
PORT	Run to whichever wall you designate as the 'Port' side.
STARBOARD	This is the opposite wall.
BOW	Imagining port as west, this is the north wall.
STERN	This is the wall opposite bow.
SCRUB THE DECKS	On hands and knees, mimic a scrubbing motion.
CLIMB THE RIGGING	Mimic a climbing motion.
SUBMARINES	Lie in the floor with a leg or arm in the air.
CAPTAIN ONBOARD	Attention and salute.
CAPTAIN'S WIFE ONDOARD	Curtsey.
BOOM COMING OVER	Duck head to below waist height.
LIFEBOATS	Get into numbered groups.

Other commands can be added, with suggestions from Scouts welcomed. Where there is a judgement to be made, the Scout judged to be last can sit out until there are only a few Scouts left and you have determined a winner.

4. In the Dark Quiz

- This game tests Scouts' observation.

- At a random and unannounced juncture in the meeting, the lights are switched off.

- Scouts are told to get in their Patrols carefully and quietly.

- Each Patrol is given one pencil and one sheet of paper.

- Ask five questions about the meeting environment. The idea is that Scouts have to be observant to notice them as there is no opportunity in the dark.

- Collect the answers in and turn the lights back on.

- This game works equally well as a Patrol Activity where Scouts are taken out of the Meeting Place and asked the questions in a room where they cannot see the answers. This variation is better suited to the summer months.

5. Pass the Light

- Split the Troop into equal teams.

- Line up rows of chairs, a chair per Scout, one metre apart.

- Each Scout stands on a chair with a dessert spoon.

- Give the first member of each team a tea light and light it.

- On the word 'GO' the tea light is placed on the first Scout's spoon and then passed down the line using only the spoons.

- Any team caught using their hands must return the tea light to the start of their line.

- The first team to pass the light to the end is the winner.

6. Bucket Ball

- Divide the young people into two even teams, which should not be more than 10 a side.

- Place a bucket at each end of the playing area and a football in the centre. The bucket is the goal for each team.

- At the start of the game each player must be holding on to their team's bucket.

- When a whistle is blown at the start of the game the players walk - not run - to the ball.

- The ball can only be passed by throwing it to a team mate and the person holding the ball can not move their feet.

- The ball is not to be knocked from someone's hands and there is to be no contact.

- If the defending team covers or moves their bucket, the attacking team automatically gets a goal.

- When goal is scored, everyone returns to their start positions.

- Play two halves of 10 minutes each.

7. Silent Bucket Ball

- This variation uses the same rules of the above game, but with no movement or talking allowed.

- At start of each round, give the Scouts five seconds to move to a new position on the pitch, where they have to stay for the rest of that round.

- Communication has to be by sign language.

- Because there is no movement, enforce the rule that at least three players in a team must pass in a chain before throwing for a goal. Otherwise the strongest Scouts in the middle will just get the ball and score from the halfway line.

8. Scout Law Relay

- Split the section into teams/Patrols.

- Place a table at either end of the Meeting Place for each Patrol.

- Scouts race from their table to collect one word at a time from the far end table.

- The first team to correctly assemble a part of the Scout law are the winners of the first round.

- Repeat until all seven parts of the Scout Law have been made. Every Scout in each Patrol should have done the relay at least twice.

Notes: For this you will need to print out each word of the Scout Law on separate cards, one copy per Patrol.

9. Piggyback Game

- Scouts randomly move around the Meeting Place.

- Shout out a number. Scouts have to form groups of the called number. Anyone without a correctly formed group gets an 'O' (Scouts continue to accumulate letters until they are O.U.T.).

- Eventually, call out the number 'two'. The Scouts then form pairs. Ask the pairs to form a circle, with the partners standing one behind the other.

- The Scouts should start in piggyback position.

- On the word 'GO' the Scouts who are mounted jump down, run clockwise round the circle back to their partner, dive under their partner's legs and then give their partner a piggyback.

- The pair who are slowest are eliminated immediately.

- Continue until you have a winning pair.

10. Chair Chase

- Set up a chair per Patrol at the far end of the Meeting Place.

- Set a chair in line with the first chair half way down the hall and place a football-size sponge ball on it.

- Scouts line up in Patrols at the near end, each facing the two chairs in line.

- The first Scout runs to the first chair, runs around it, then picks up the ball and throws it at the chair at the end of the hall.

- Once they have hit the chair with the ball they replace the ball on the first chair and run to the back of their team. If they miss they must pick up the ball, return to the throwing chair, and throw again.

- The next player goes, and so on until the whole Patrol have had their turn.

- The first team to finish wins.

11. Shoe Hunt

- Scouts remove their shoes and pile them in the middle of the Meeting Place.

- With the young people facing the wall, mix up the shoes.

- Turn the lights off.

- Scouts have to find their own shoes within a set time (two minutes works well).

- All those without at least one of their shoes is then 'out' and the game is repeated with those still in until you have a winner.

Note: This game can become boisterous. Brief the Scouts beforehand so that accidents are prevented.

12. Nobody's Airship

- Two teams sit in two rows facing each other, knees about a foot from those of the opposite team.

- A balloon is thrown in, both teams pat it with their hands to keep it in the air and try to send it far over the heads of their opponents.

- If it falls to the ground behind one team, they lose a point.

- The game is best of five points, then start a new match.

13. Cat and Mouse

- Pair the Troop up. Each pair should link arms.

- All the pairs stand in a large circle, facing in. The pairs should not be able to touch each other - there should be gaps large enough that people can run through them.

- Select one pair to start the game as 'cat' and 'mouse', i.e. one hunter and one hunted.

- The aim of the game is that the cat must try to catch the mouse:

  - The mouse can escape by running around the area, in and out of the other pairs in the circle.

  - The cat may only run around the outside of the circle.

- The mouse is caught if touched by the cat. However, the mouse may also escape by linking arms with one of the players standing as a pair in the circle. If this happens, the player on the other side of the pair becomes the mouse and must try and escape the cat.

- If the mouse is caught, the mouse then becomes the cat - the hunter becomes the hunted - and must try and escape in the manner described above.

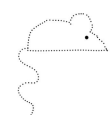

14. The News Quiz

- Split the Section into teams or Patrols.

- Give each team a copy of the same newspaper (keep one for yourself).

- Call out questions and a clue to where the answer is in the newspaper (a headline, the price of a car from a certain garage, what time a certain TV programme is on, a telephone number for the weather helpline, etc).

- The first team to get the answer wins a point.

- At the end, the team with the most points wins.

Hint: A tip for the teams is to split the papers up and spread them out. The first team to get it back into order gets an extra points (a good way to get tidy up quickly at the end!)

15. Wink Murder

- Scouts sit in a circle.

- One is chosen to be the detective. They leave the room.

- The remaining Scouts close their eyes. With eyes closed, walk around the outside of the circle, patting one Scout on the head. They will be the murderer. Walk around twice to build the suspense if required.

- The detective comes in. The objective of the murderer is to murder everyone by winking at them. The detective's goal is to catch the murderer before everybody dies.

- The detective has three guesses. Once a verdict is reached, another Scout is sent out as the detective and the game can continue as long as desired.

Note: It is customary to encourage over the top and dramatic deaths, with extra points for noise and individuality!

16. Circle Dodgeball

- Draw a large circle on the floor in the centre of the Meeting Place.

- One Patrol is sent into the circle. The other Patrols stand around the outside of the circle and throw footballs at those inside.

- A hit below the knee is out.

- The winner from each Patrol goes into a final at the end of the game.

Note: This game brings with it an intriguing conundrum: the Scouts must work together in the first round to ensure a good showing, but they are also competing against each other to get into the final. You could discuss how they are able to do their best in this circumstance.

17. Four Goal Football

- Set up a football pitch (outdoors) with four goals at the cardinal compass points instead of the usual two.

- Split the Section into four equal teams, who must each defend one goal.

- Start with two balls. Introduce more as the game goes on.

- Play to the normal rules of football, with four periods of five minutes.

- Each team has one player that counts the goals conceded. The team with the least goals conceded is announced after each period. This should mean that the other teams attack their goal in the next period.

- Continue to add up the scores, introduce more balls, switch players, until the final whistle.

- The team that has conceded fewest goals is the winner.

18. Three Step Tag

- This variation requires a little more thought than usual from the players.

- Define the playing area. Don't make it too big or the game takes too long. You'll need to spread the players about two to three metres apart at the most.

- Choose someone to do the catching. With a small group use only one, but it works better with more in bigger groups. Blindfold the catcher(s).

- Everyone finds a spot in the playing area and stands still.

- The catchers are released into the playing area and have to find the players to catch them. Remind the players that silence makes them hard to find.

- To avoid being caught, the players are allowed to take only three steps in the whole game. They may bend or crouch or lie down. One roll on the floor counts as one step.

- Be as mean or as lenient as you want.

- The game finishes when all (or nearly all) have been caught.

19. Chairball

- This is a simple game where the aim is to defend your chair.

- Each Scout gets a chair and places it in the playing area, standing next to it.

- Throw a soft sponge ball into the playing area.

- Scouts try to stop their chair being hit by kicking the ball away from it. They can also try to hit opponents' chairs.

- Using arms is not allowed but they can block with the rest of the body.

- Once a chair has been hit, the Scout defending it sits on their chair and is out. They can continue to kick the ball when it comes near.

- The winner is the last Scout standing.

20. Duck and Egg

- Scouts stand in a circle, facing in.

- Stand in the middle of the circle holding a ball (the egg) and a plastic duck.

- Pass the duck to any Scout. This is then passed continuously around the circle.

- Next throw the ball at random to any Scout (while the duck is going around). Whoever catches the ball has to throw it back to the centre.

- If either the duck or egg is dropped then that Scout is out and sits down, still in the circle, (the size of the circle does not decrease). The remaining players have to pass the duck around over the 'out' players heads and still try to catch the egg at the same time.

- The winner is the last Scout standing.

Note: The game can be made more complicated by using more than one egg or duck at once. Try it with two eggs and two ducks going in different directions!

21. Kangaroo Sumo

- Lay a rope circle of about four diameter (depending on Troop size) to form the playing area (Use chalk as an alternative)

- Number the Scouts off and to begin the game call out two numbers.

- The two Scouts called cross their arms and hop to the middle of the ring.

- The object of the game is to either knock the opponent over or bump them out of the ring without putting the other foot on the floor or uncrossing the arms.

- Towards the end of the game call out more than two numbers!

Note: This is a physical game that can be rough, so be sensible when matching opponents, and watch each bout closely. Play the game on a soft surface.

22. Pass the Keys

- All Scouts sit in a circle.

- One Scout goes into the middle and closes their eyes.

- The Scouts in the circle start to pass the keys (or similar object) around the circle.

- The Scout in the middle claps their hands. At this point the keys must stop moving.

- Without looking up the Scout in the centre says a letter of the alphabet.

- The Scout with the keys passes the keys around the circle and tries to say ten words beginning with that letter before the keys are back in their hands.

- Fails - choose another Scout to go in the middle.

- Succeeds - Scout stays in the middle.

Notes: You may need to vary the number of words to make the game easier or harder. Also, you will have to stop the use of difficult letters (i.e. 'x') as these will be obvious choices to start with.

23. Triangles

- Gather all the Scouts in the Meeting Place.

- Get them to run around randomly to begin with. Then after a few seconds, shout 'freeze.'

- In their heads, the Scouts have to pick two other Scouts without making any signal of who they have picked.

- The aim of the game is now explained. You have to try and stand in a position where you are the same distance from each the two Scouts you picked. This forms an equilateral triangle (all the sides the same length).

- The game should be played in silence. It will become clear that it is nigh on impossible, and just as you think you are getting close, one of the 'corners' will move.

Note: This is the kind of game you can play with the Troop from time to time, to see if they improve in the way they approach it.

24. What Are You Doing?

- Scout stand in a large circle, facing in.

- The first Scout comes into the circle and starts doing an obvious action, such as washing a car. Pause to watch the action for a few seconds. Then point at another Scout in the circle. They ask 'What are you doing?'

- The Scout in the middle has to give an answer that is anything but what they were doing, for example 'I'm laying an egg.'

- The Scout who asked the question now goes into the centre, and has to perform the action stated, i.e. laying an egg.

- The game continues with the action constantly changing. Quick-witted Scouts will suggest some hilarious actions, and you may need to use the veto on occasion. This dramatic game should help to bring people out of their shell!

25. Riskit

- This is a simple dice game requiring nerve and judgment, best played in a small group.

- Each Scout takes a turn rolling one dice. If they roll a two, three, four, five or six. They roll again and their score accumulates. They can choose to quit rolling at any stage, and their total score is recorded, thus ending their turn.

- If they roll a one, they lose all their points and their turn is over.

- Play in rounds, with the first to five wins the overall champion.

- How far will you Riskit?

26. Eddylong Ball

- Indoor ball game played in teams:

- Divide the Troop into two teams, one batting and the other fielding.

- The batting team line up against a wall. The fielding team occupy the playing area.

- A bowler is nominated and throws underarm towards the batter's head (there is no wicket).

- The batter has to head the ball into the field of play and run to the opposite wall without getting caught or hit below the knee with the ball. If they get to the opposite wall without any of these things happening, they are safe.

- To score a point, the runner has to make it back to their team's wall without being hit. They can only run when the ball is in play.

- A runner can stay on the safe side of the hall for as long as they want, until there is only one batter left.

- If there is only one batter left then they must make it to the safe wall and back again to score a point.

- Players that are out have to sit down on their team's wall.

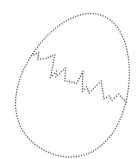

APPENDIX – RESOURCES

The Aviation Skills Quiz (Term 3, week 7)

Parts of the aircraft (Term 3, week 7)

Make a balsa glider (Term 3, week 7)

Route plan 1 and 2 (Term 2, week 7)

The Aviation Skills Quiz

Insert into the definitions the correct words from the list in the box below. The number of spaces matches the number of letters in the words. Use that to help you label the aeroplane diagrams, again using the words from the box below. Some words will be used more than once on the diagram.

The left side of an aircraft is called _ _ _ _   It·is thought it got this name from ancient ships which had the steering device on the right side of the ship. The ship could therefore only enter the harbour or port on the side that did not have the steering mechanism.

The fixed vertical part of the tail is called the _ _ _ . It provides stability, and has a movable control surface attached to it.

The front of an aircraft is called the _ _ _ _ .

This part of the aeroplane lifts and carries the aeroplane when flying. To take-off and climb, the _ _ _ _ must produce more lift than the aircraft's total weight. Lift is generated by increasing the speed of air flowing over the top of the _ _ _ _ (use the same word again).

The body of an aeroplane is called the _ _ _ _ _ _ _ _ . It holds the wing and tail in position, enabling the aeroplane to fly correctly.

The _ _ _ _ _ are attached to the trailing edge (back) of the wing near the fuselage. When in use, they increase the area and angle of the wing. This increases lift and makes take-off easier and landing safer.

The _ _ _ _ _ _ is attached to the fin, and is connected to pedals in the cockpit. The pilot uses the pedals to move it to the left or right. This changes the way the air flows over it, and aids the pilot in steering the aeroplane left or right.

The _ _ _ _ _ _ _ _ is the fixed horizontal part of the tail. It provides stability, and has a movable control surface attached to it.

The right side of an aircraft is called _ _ _ _ _ _ _ _ _ . The words comes from the original word 'Steerboard' a steering device used on ancient ships which was always on the right side of the boat.

The _ _ _ _ _ _ _ _ _ are attached to the tailplane, and are connected to the control column in the cockpit. The pilot moves the control column backward or forward to move them up or down. This changes the way the air flows over them, and aids the pilot in steering the aeroplane up or down.

The _ _ _ _ _ _ _ _ are attached to the trailing edge of the wing near the wing tips, and are connected to the control column in the cockpit. The pilot moves the control column to the left or right to move them up or down (if one is up, the other is always down). This changes the way the air flows over them, and aids the pilot to roll (tilt) the aircraft .

| Port | Elevators | Wing(Mainplane) | Fuselage | Nose | Ailerons |
| Tailplane | Fin | Starboard | Rudder | Flaps | |

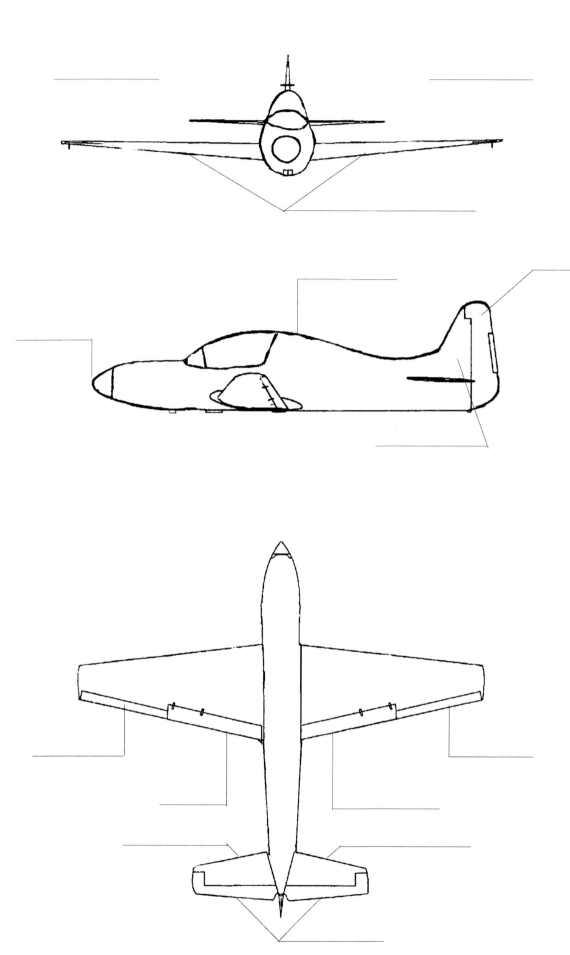

You can find more resources to deliver the Basic Aviation Skills Activity Badge at IWM Duxford online at http://duxford.iwm.org.uk

Balsa Glider

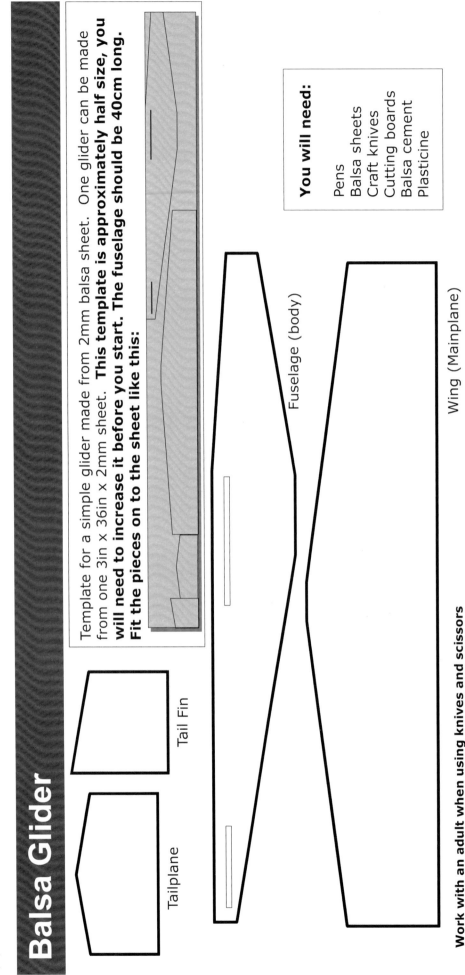

Template for a simple glider made from 2mm balsa sheet. One glider can be made from one 3in x 36in x 2mm sheet. **This template is approximately half size, you will need to increase it before you start. The fuselage should be 40cm long. Fit the pieces on to the sheet like this:**

Tail Fin

Tailplane

Fuselage (body)

Wing (Mainplane)

You will need:

Pens
Balsa sheets
Craft knives
Cutting boards
Balsa cement
Plasticine

Work with an adult when using knives and scissors

1. Draw round the template onto the balsa sheet

2. Carefully cut out the shapes using a craft knife. Cut using lots of small, short cuts. DO NOT press hard or try to cut out using long deep cuts - you are likely to cut yourself!

3. Cut out the slots in the fuselage.

4. Gently push the tailplane and wing through the slots on the fuselage

5. Glue the fin onto the fuselage (following the instructions on the balsa cement)

6. Use the plasticine on the nose of the glider to balance it.

7. Test fly the glider. If it dives remove some weight. If it climbs and stalls add some weight.